The Ur-Board Book

Walt Darring

I0487974

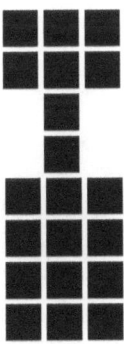

WWW.Lulu.com

Lulu Enterprises, Inc

The Ur-Board Book
by Walt Darring

Copyright © 2010

www.Lulu.com
Lulu Enterprises, Inc.

ISBN: 978-0-557-49490-3

I would like to express my thanks for the help and support I received from friends and relatives, especially my wife Jean and our children, grandchildren, and great-grandchildren, my brothers Gerald and Mike, and a few Ur-board enthusiasts— Fred Marchman, Alan Beall, Roy Randall, et al.

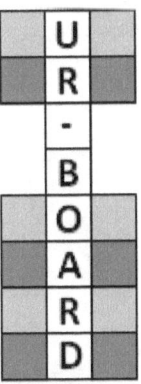

Dedicated
to my helpmates,
Jean and Jerry

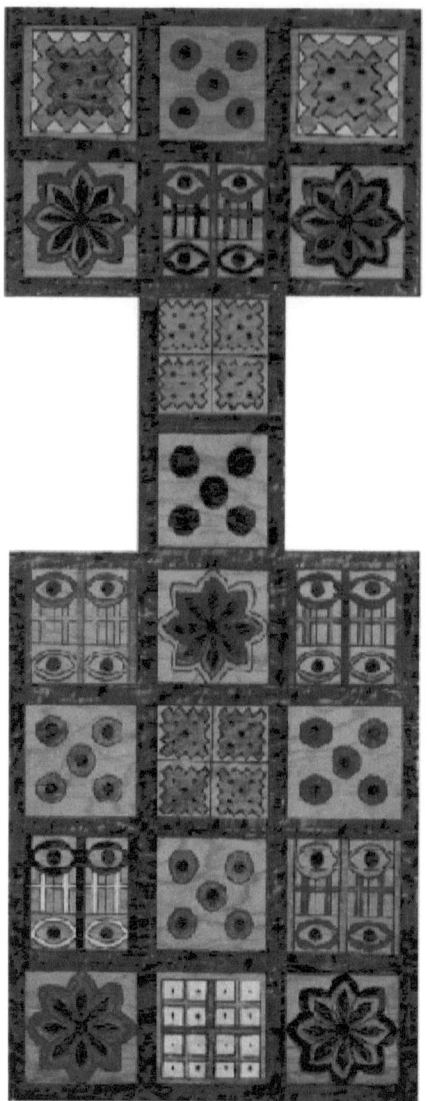

Photo by Gordon Beall.

The Wizard's Ur-Board

Created in 1968, this game board was the setting for the Ur-games played during the time when they were being discovered. It was painted in water color on thin plyboard, outlined with a woodburner, and varnished.

The Ur-Board Book
by Walt Darring

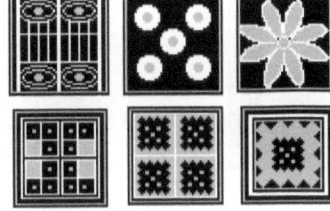

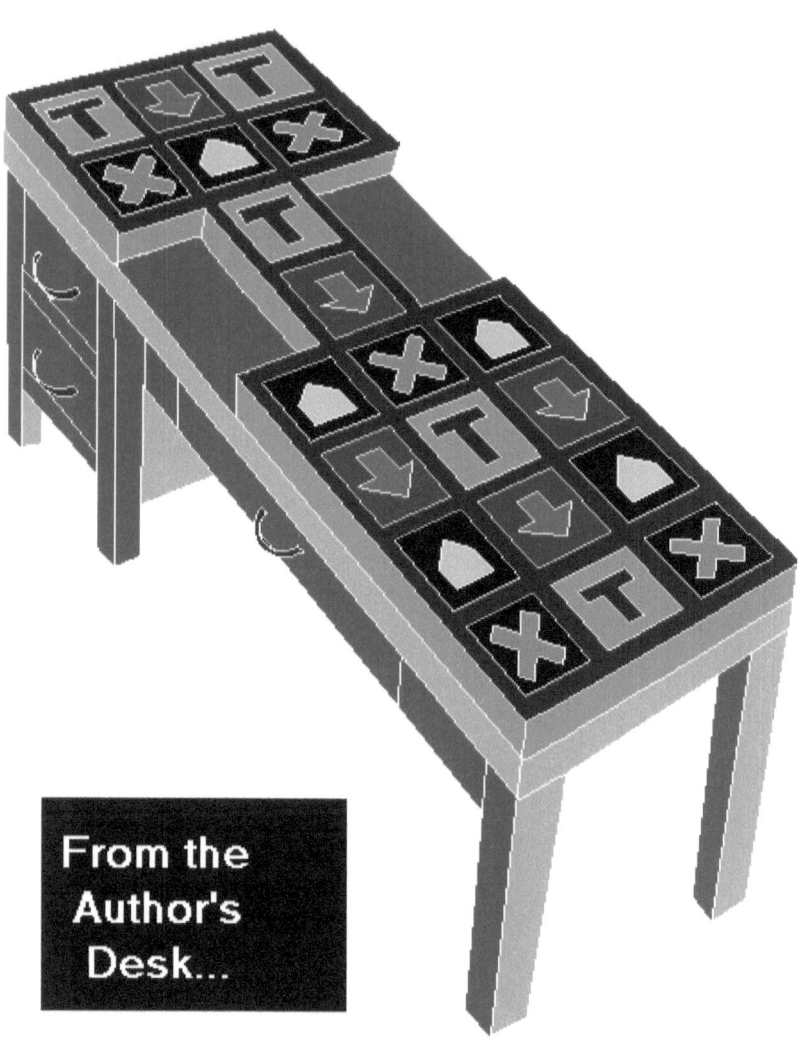

From the
Author's
Desk...

The Ur-Board Book

The Ur-Board Book

The Ur-Board Book

The Ur-Board Book

The Ur-Board Book

The Ur-Board Book

The Ur-Board Book

In the late 1920's, Sir Leonard Woolley led an archeological expedition in the Near East to a strip of river delta and arid desert in modern Iraq, once known as Sumer (or more properly, Shumer). The league of cities clustered about its rivers was already ancient when the writers of *Genesis* mentioned it by name as "Shinar," land of the mighty hunter Nimrod, whose kingdom included Babel, Erech, and Akkad. But beyond this brief mention in the Bible, little was known of the old pre-Babylonian culture. Only in 1869 were the names of "Sumer" and its people, the "Sumerians," restored to history, via the newly deciphered language inscribed in clay. Woolley, following up on the hints of scholars, carefully excavated the mounds in southern Iraq and uncovered the ruins of the world's first cities. There, in the royal tombs of Ur and neighboring sites, he found a hoard of treasures—artifacts of gold and lapis lazuli, as well as countless clay tablets with cuneiform writing.

Among these treasures were game boards which came to be known as "the Royal Game of Ur." Their design, made of shell and lapis lazuli, had been laid out on a wooden base, below which was a drawer with dice and markers in it; but the wood had long ago disappeared, and the fragile tiles lay embedded in the clay. Woolley poured wax over the design, lifted it intact, and set it on a new wooden base without having to reconstruct the design. Had the boards been discovered just a few decades earlier, they would likely have been scattered by the crude digging practices of past ages and, after four and a half millennia of fortunate survival, been lost to the world at last.

For some of these tombs had not been looted by grave robbers in the thousands of years of their existence. Why they had been spared the fate of so many ancient grave sites in the Near East was but one of many mysteries that would emerge from this archeological project.

Even more puzzling were the great antiquity of Sumerian culture and the high level of civilization they had achieved. Sumer was older than Egypt, India, and all other known civilizations. The oldest city of Sumer, Eridu, had been built upon a thin foundation of pre-historic development, beneath which was nothing but primordial earth. Yet with the discovery and deciphering of the clay tablets, when historians entered at last into the dark millennium before the age of Homer and Moses, they found therein the prototypes of the Hebrew myths of *Genesis,* and an epic poem similar to the *Odyssey*, about the adventures of Gilgamesh, the hero-king of Erech. They also found a body of laws pre-dating Hammurabi by several centuries, and evidence of astonishing innovations associated with higher and much later civilizations. The eminent Sumerologist, Samuel N. Kramer, listed (in his book *History Begins at Sumer),* twenty-seven of history's "firsts," among which were the first schools, where students were taught the complex skills of writing with a stylus on clay tablets; they also memorized the rules of grammar, and a whole dictionary of terms— the names of many kinds of birds, fishes, insects, trees, minerals, and metals; and they recited classic works of poetry, solved mathematical problems, and studied astronomy, biology, botany, geography, and linguistics. The young scribes were given a "university" education. Among other firsts were a bicameral congress, that shared power with the king; a medical profession that prescribed herbal and mineral remedies of all sorts, and surgeons that performed delicate surgical operations; a farmer's almanac and handbook; wisdom books of proverbs, fables, literary debates, and other ethical teachings; recipes for the preparation of elegant cuisine; myths of Paradise, the Flood, the Underworld, and a Golden Age of peace and happiness, all of which formed the basis of the revealed religions of the West.

Here was a full-blown advanced civilization, sprung from little or no past history! Even today, many people on Earth live with much less knowledge, refinement, and social organization than the Sumerians enjoyed; yet they were but a few centuries removed from the wild conditions of hunters and gatherers.

And there were other inexplicable mysteries, of larger scope and consequence— such as: who *were* the Sumerians, the "black-haired people," as they were called? They had no racial predecessors. And how can we account for the condition they found themselves in, the "Garden of Eden" (situated, the Bible says, between the Tigris and Euphrates rivers), which science has shown to be the source of all agricultural vegetation (grains, fruits, and plants) and domestic animals (dogs, cattle, goats, and swine) on Earth, a development which occurred soon after the end of the Ice Age, and spread throughout the world from the environs of the Near East? These questions were raised more than half a century after Woolley's expedition, by Zecharia Sitchin, a Sumerologist who, by then, was able to read enough of the inscribed stones and clay tablets to get a wholly new version of the origins of civilization— based on the testimony of the Sumerians themselves.

As the earliest Sumerological studies made clear, the ancient Sumerians believed that their purpose on earth was "to serve the gods." They also claimed that the gods had taught them everything, including agriculture and metalurgy, the calendar and the zodiac, mathematics and architecture. To modern scholars, these claims seemed merely to describe their indebtedness to the sort of divinities we are familiar with— supernatural spirits, knowable only through faith. But Sitchin's work on the ancient Babylonian theogony, the *Enuma Elish,* that described the formation of the Solar System, and his studies of Bible stories in the light of Sumerian lore, have convinced some scholars that the Sumerian "gods" were real people, called the Anunnaki, who came to Earth from a planet within our system; that they "created" the human race by genetic engineering, uniting their own seed with that of a breed of primates which they had found living in Africa; that "The Adam" was the first successful hybrid, and Eve's genes perhaps were taken from his rib. Later, after the Biblical Flood destroyed the Anunnaki's original space colony, they returned and built the pyramids of Gizeh and the Sphinx (about twelve thousand years ago) as part of their new space port on Earth. Sitchin said that the gods taught the Sumerians (and the Egyptians and Hindus, and the Incas and Mayans) the ways of civilized life (kingship and bureaucracy) and scientific thought (the 360 degree circle, and the precession of the equinoxes). But eventually, he said, the gods fought among themselves (as recorded in the *Baghavad Gita*) and dropped nuclear bombs on Earth, destroying Sodom and Gomorrah, and in one final immense explosion annihilating the huge space station on the Arabian Peninsula— after which, the radiation from that blast drifted downwind and, with silent and eerie suddenness, poisoned and killed the entire population of the city of Ur. Scarcely a single person survived. The destruction was so mysterious and so complete, that no one, it seems, dared to dig through or enter those poisoned tombs, until the cursed cities of Sumer had been covered over by Time and lost to History.

This is a strange and radical revision for scientists to verify and incorporate into the history of human origins; but the scholarship is sound, and the new version of events would solve many of the mysteries surrounding Sumer and the early history of Mankind. The intervention of the gods explains, for instance, the sudden proliferation of domestic plants and animals in the earliest phases of the Agricultural revolution, just in time for Mankind to make use of them. It also explains the mysterious condition of the human genome, in which the second and third genes, it is said, seem to have been fused or spliced by someone manipulating the microscopic development. And it accounts for the special way in which human organs, muscles, and skin evolved, unlike those of other primates that lived alongside them on the African savannah. And finally, it helps explain the great antiquity of the Gizeh monuments, as indicated by the erosion of the Sphinx, and the astronomical alignment of the pyramids.

*　*　*　*　*

My interest in the mysteries of Sumer began in 1968, when I found a life-size color print of the "Royal Game of Ur" in the Spring issue of *Horizon* Magazine. I knew little about the Sumerian/Akkadian civilization, except that it was very primitive and would probably be of little interest to me, as a student of symbolism. Archaic symbolism is often obscure and superstitious. But here, in this game board from Ur, there were very distinct characters, overtly symbolic, and arranged in symbolic patterns on the board. Immediately I knew I must have a copy of that curious design. So, cutting a strip of ply board to size and shape, I penciled in the designs, painted them in water colors, outlined all images with a wood-burner, and covered the board with a coat of varnish. Thus, a half a century ago, I created my first Ur-board. It is hanging on the wall of my studio, looking over my shoulder at this very moment.

It used to hang out in the living room, where it observed our family meals and customs. Our friends talked to us about this symbolic design. They liked it as a work of art, but couldn't help asking: *What does it mean? Anything? Or just whatever you want*?

In response to this demand, I developed a number of credible interpretations, to entertain and astonish my friends. And in no time at all, the Ur-board became a cult figure among us. Its analogies hardened into categories: History arose, Art ensued, Philosophy reigned a while; and then emerged the Archetypes of Religion— and the surprising intimations of Prophecy. I don't know when play left off and serious business began (perhaps never), but it became apparent at some point that the messages I was getting by interpreting the symbolism of the Ur-board were beautifully and impressively meaningful.

This was my early relationship with the mystic game board. For two years, my friends and I did nothing with the Ur-board but sit around, from time to time, and talk about it. Then one day we took it down from the wall and played our first Ur-board game, using four dice and fourteen Mardi Gras doubloons, seven silver and seven gold. We rolled and moved the markers, jumping on and off the board, agreeing and disagreeing on the rules as we made them up.

That was it; the games changed everything. We had the Ur-board in our hands almost every day. We studied the design, letting it suggest the arrangement of markers and the rules of play. There were "chase" games, two sides racing along a common path, knocking opponents aside. And there were "placement" games, when numbers had been assigned to the suits, numbers that could be rolled on a cubic die. And there were "conflict" games, cops and robbers, a Wild West shootout, ancient battle scenes. And there were paper games, and party games, and much more.

* * * * *

It was originally my intention to study the civilization of Sumer and discover in its art some clue to the meanings of the Ur-board symbols. *What*, I asked, *did the Ur-board mean to the people who invented it and played games with it?* But that seemed to me to be asking too much, to study an entire civilization and a thousand years of history in order to understand a single object? Why not the other way? Why not study the object to find out what the civilization was like. The job would be simpler, and the ideas easier to understand. I would be asking, *What does the Ur-board mean to us?*

Besides, what had impressed me and my friends most was not the ancient culture of Ur, but the categorical arrangement of symbols on the Ur-board, like icons on the computer, which could be shown to represent significant ideas, thoughts that mattered to a modern viewer.

Psychology had taught me to look upon "symbols" (the stuff of dreams and art) as the vocabulary of the imagination; for properly understood, the symbols of dreams speak to us with clarity and precision, and they teach us what we unconsciously believe. All we need to have is the Common Sense to recognize analogous realities, and an Ironic Mind to perceive elements of wit and meaning in them. From my work with literary criticism, I discovered that one can interpret symbolic images and allegorical narratives with a great deal of confidence; and that if one can explain symbols with clarity and conviction, you won't have to be a philosopher or psychologist to appreciate and agree with the interpretation. The key to it all is allegorical structure, the structure of an art-form, as a context for its symbols.

It was in this spirit that I had begun to discuss the meaning of the Ur-board. But I was in for a surprise. For I had conceived of the job in its beginning as interpreting a message from the prehistoric past, a message communicated by pictorial designs because as yet there was no writing. Furthermore, to begin with, I anticipated hearing from the archetypal mind of a primitive shaman, from the depths of savage instinct, from the wisdom of simple feeling. But that was not what I found in the Sumerian game board. The Ur-board "conversed" meaningfully about history, philosophy, civilization, and other modern concerns. It seemed implausible that primitive star-gazers and tribal priests from the beginning of history— that such an early, inexperienced intelligence could have created this paradigm of Thought.

And that is where the new Sumerology of Zecharia Sitchin came into play. The minds of recently evolved *homo sapiens* could not have created or understood the Ur-board— but the higher intelligence of alien beings, many millennia older than we are today, certainly could have.

Judging from when and where it was found, the Ur-board must have been for its owners a "sacred" object, given them by the gods. To commemorate that event, a new Ur-board, perhaps, was presented by the high priest to each new king of Ur as he took the throne; and the dead king's Ur-board was buried with him. But we do not know how the board was used. It may have been used for play in the king's court, for gambling among the lords, or for divination by the temple magicians. However it was used, the priests of Ur apparently venerated the Ur-board and considered it an indispensable instrument for the *lugal* after he was dead, to accompany him in the Underworld.

⁑

Part 1:

A Symbolic Analysis of the Ur-Board

by Walt Darring

The following pages present an interpretation of the Royal Game of Ur, based on an analysis of its symbols and structures. This is a modern interpretation. I do not pretend to know what Sumerians meant or understood by these formal devices; but symbols from other cultures, when they are analogous to the forms of nature and observe patterns of rational thought, can have readily recognizable meanings. And if the structural context of the symbol is known, it can speak to a modern symbolist in the universal language of symbolism, about things not thought to be known when the symbols were created. This claim can be proved, not by scientific or scholarly standards, but by the conviction of an unbiased reader, when the correspondence between things and ideas seems plausible and clear. So, Reader, judge for yourself. If you are persuaded, I am content. History is on our side.

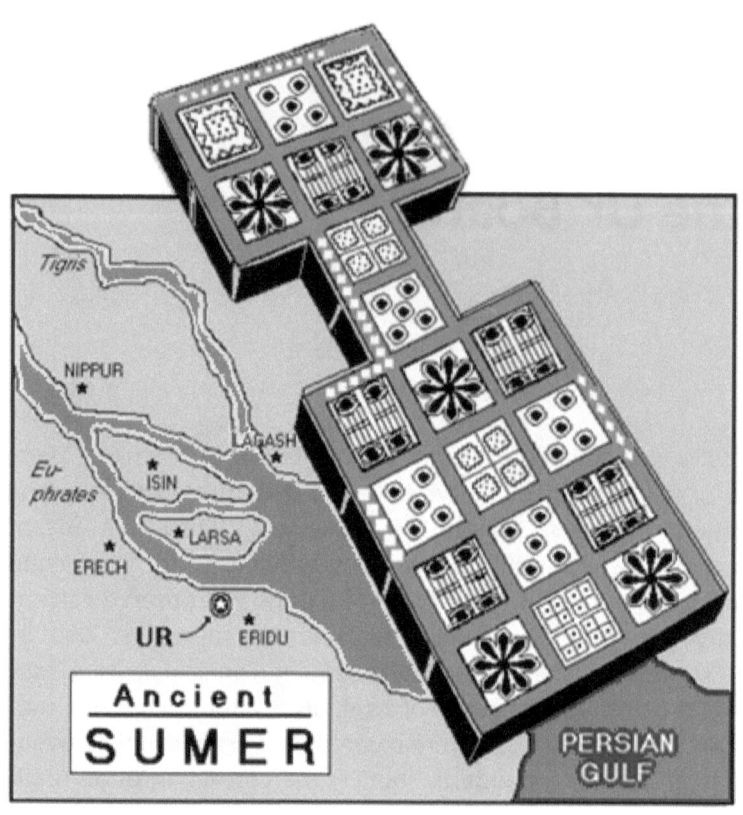

The ROYAL GAME of UR

1. The Royal Game of Ur

The original Ur-board looks like a piece of miniature furniture, ornate but somewhat crudely crafted from expensive materials. The game board design is laid out in tiles on the surface of a small, flat, wooden chest about a foot in length, with a drawer entering at the bottom of the board. The drawer holds six pyramid-shaped dice and fourteen markers, seven black and seven white. A curious antique, and a valuable museum piece, in its own day it was merely a household object, like the game boards we keep in our closets.

Nevertheless, even the first impression of the Ur-board can be striking and memorable— not just for its beauty, but for its mystery and meaning as well. It has a curious appeal to our intellect; its anthropomorphic structure engages our attention, like a person standing before us; its complement of symbols— the eyes, the flowers, the coins— seem meaningful.

What, we wonder, might the Ur-board be trying to tell us? What message from the infant race of Adam and Eve? Or what might the gods have been saying to our forefathers by giving them the Ur-board? What royal wisdom did they hope to impart to their former clones and slaves to prepare them for self-rule?

These thoughts are religious in nature. And after all, being Ancient, Biblical, and Chaldean, the Ur-board could hardly be expected to refrain from speaking to us about the First Things of religion. But as the oldest game board on Earth, the Ur-board may embody the inscrutable wisdom of ancient shamans or magi, so that even if she did speak, we might not understand her.

But as it turns out, that isn't so. The Ur-board isn't arcane or inscrutable. She's smart, and clever, and above all— modern! Her symbols speak to us in our idiom and address our concerns.

But before we begin to investigate this symbolic artifact, we must ask: What do we have here? What do we refer to when we speak of the Ur-Board? Is it the object in the museum, something we can touch? Or is it an idea derived from a number of similar boards, known collectively by that name?

It is both. For there is the one true Ur-board, and there are two of her. Let me explain.

Upside Down Tiles
in Two Extant
Sumerian Gameboards

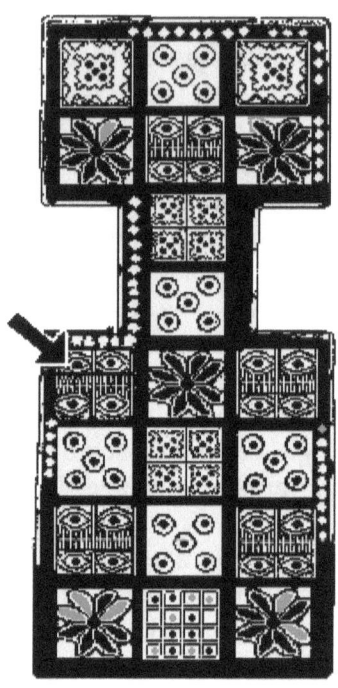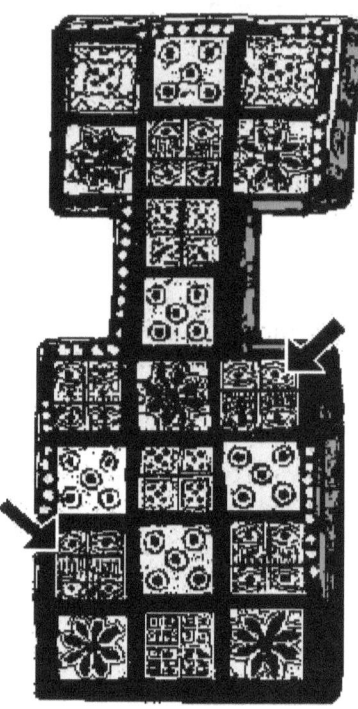

These illustrations are taken from published photos of the ancient artifacts,
touched up on Paint to clarify the designs and suggest the condition of the boards.

2. Two Identical Game Boards from Ur

Pictured here are two small wooden game boards which were discovered in the royal tombs of Ur. They had been buried with kings of the Third Dynasty of Ur, around 2,500 B.C.

Though these boards were found in different tombs, they are identical in all respects, with the same kind and number of dice and markers buried with them. This seems to indicate that the design of the board was rigidly prescribed, and intended to survive the centuries in exactly the same form. Their twenty tiles are identical in design and arrangement— with one exception.

Notice that the "eyes-at-the-gates" design is the only symbol on the board that has a distinct top and bottom; the rest are symmetrical, horizontally and vertically. Now if you're not paying attention when you make an Ur-board, you can place that tile upside down. And that is what seems to have happened with both game boards; the artisans got them wrong, and in different places. The British Museum Ur-board (left) has an upside down tile on the right shoulder of the board; the other Ur-board has two wrong tiles, one on the right hand and one on the left shoulder. These are not disturbing irregularities; you scarcely notice them. In fact, that may be the reason the mistakes were made. But it is very strange. These were treasured artifacts of the king. Wouldn't the artists who made them be sure to check every detail of their design? Was this a symptom of decadence in the middle of the third millennium BC— namely, that the Ur-board, which had been preserved by centuries of devotion, should fall into disuse and neglect, such that the artist working on it would not know he was putting tiles in upside down?

For in making Ur-boards for two different kings, and for two different tombs, they had faithfully observed the specifications of a plan; and in many other things (temples, cities, ziggurats) the gods had given men simple but explicit instructions for how to make or build them. So, it is credible to suppose that at an early date in the history of Sumer, the gods had given the first kings, not a board, but instructions for making one; and the Sumerians had preserved that wisdom as their priestly heritage.

ROOMS. . YELLOW
COINS . . . GREEN
GATES . . . BLUE
FLOWERS. . RED

The
Ur-Board

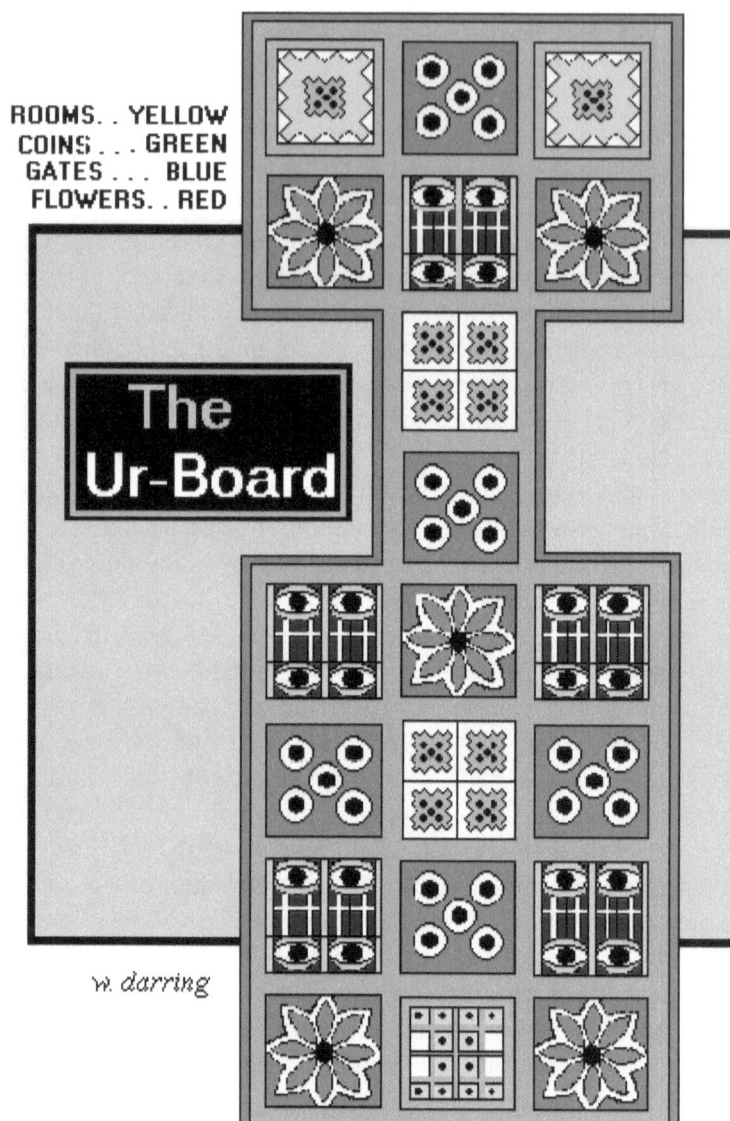

w. darring

3. The Ur-Board

In similar fashion, I will not make and market an Ur-board for you to study and play games on. Instead, I will, like the very gods, give you plain and simple directions for making an Ur-board, and let you make a board for yourself. In the course of reading this book, you will discover why that is the best way to proceed.

The beauty of any particular Ur-board resides in the interplay between the medium and the spirit. This one is made entirely of pixels, stained with Paint. The clarity and freshness of this design allows you to see it as a modern artifact, youthful in spirit and ready to play. We have added colors to the designs and names to the suits, to help you perceive the formal elements of the design; but in this edition of the Ur-Board Book, all colors are represented as shades of gray. So you must imagine the difference. But first:

Observe the Form.

Familiarize yourself with its design.

It has four "suits" of symbols, each with five tiles:

    a) the **Flowers,** in Red, forming an X on the board;

    b) the **Gates**, in Blue, forming a House;

    c) the **Coins**, in Green, forming an Arrow; and

    d) the abstract **Rooms** designs, in Yellow, forming a Tree.

These are the four suits in the ancient Ur-board.

There are strong and weak designs among the suits. The strong suits dominate the board, visually. Often the first impression a person gets from the Ur-board is: "It seems to be looking back at me." It's the eyes, of course— ten pairs of eyes arranged over the board. The eyes of the Gates suit give the Ur-board a knowing air.

You'd have to look closely at an Ur-board to see how many Rooms or Coins there are. Not so the Flowers. There are five of them, forming a giant X. Esthetically, this very conspicuous suit has a most pleasing effect, as if it braced and stabilized the head. It seems functional, as well as decorative.

Gates and Flowers are the dominant suits. In play, they will be Trumps.

Rooms are the "center of attention," running vertically the length of the board. They seem to present us with a symbolic pattern, in three parts, like the plot of a story. But visually, they are a weak suit.

Coins are even less conspicuous. You have to search for them, sometimes. They are the Odd Suit.

The Six Symbols on
the Sumerian Ur-Board

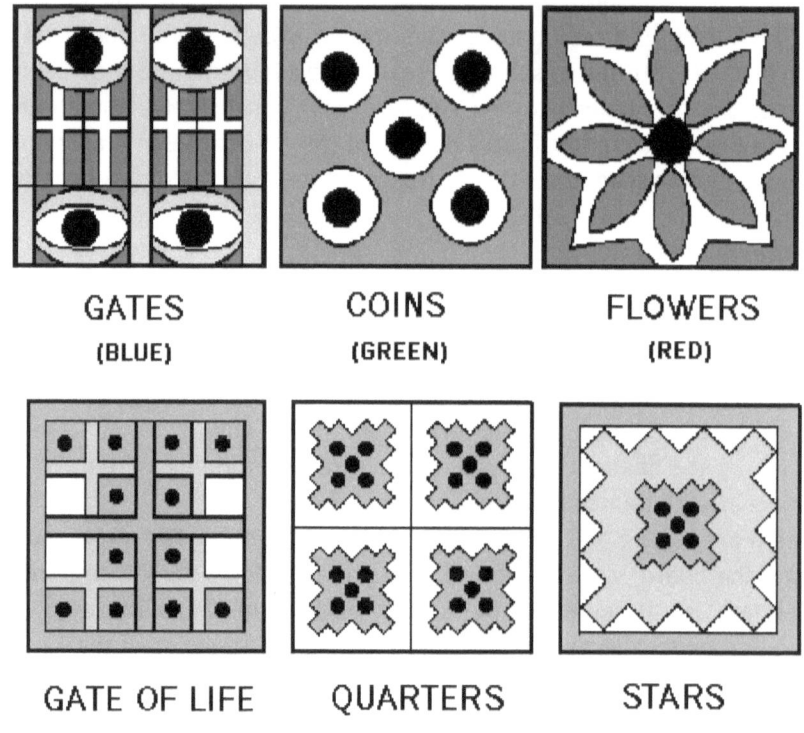

GATES
(BLUE)

COINS
(GREEN)

FLOWERS
(RED)

GATE OF LIFE

QUARTERS

STARS

ROOMS Suit

(TWO SHADES OF YELLOW)

4. The Six Tile Symbols

Notice that the tile designs are not obscure like magic runes, or primitive like the images of animals in cave art. They are Romantic symbols— Gates and Coins and Flowers! They are simple but evocative, bold and yet modest.

Let us take the **Gates** design first, because it is the most primitive, a pictographic symbol. It represents a city in siege. Watching at the gates was an important part of life in ancient Sumer, with the enemy below tirelessly working to undermine the city's foundation. Or Gates may be a scene of imprisonment, the guards at the gates, watching over the prisoners below. Or it may represent the Living, ever vigilant, and the Dead, awake in their graves below.

It stands for all of them, together. For Gates symbolize the "separation" that exists in human nature. The eyes above the gates are those of Consciousness; the eyes below are those of Conscience. In this separated condition, Conscience seems to besiege Consciousness, threatening it with moral judgment; and therefore Consciousness imprisons Conscience, so it can't prevent us from doing what we want. Thus we are separated within ourselves. This separation reflects our universal condition, for the human race exists in a divided state: some of us are to be found among the Living, others sleep among the Dead; and the Gates of Birth and Death are forever closed between us.

In contrast to this sacred view of life, **Coins** symbolize secular experience as a means of facilitating change in one's life. It represents the "ex-change" of values, by which we learn from each other. In it we see the four-cornered world of Gates, united by a central point, the Ego, forming an x.

Flowers are a symbol of flowering beauty, beauty that emerges from within, as in the blossoming of a person's character. The eight petals of the flower form an "an" sign, the first letter of the first alphabet of Man, used to identify a god in the clay inscriptions of Sumer.

Rooms, the yellow suit, is divided into three separate symbols: the first, at the bottom of the board, (called the **Gate of Life)** consists of a cross-of-crosses; the second, in the middle of the board, (called **Quarters)** is a cross-of-Xes; and the third one, at the top of the board (called **Stars)** is an X-of-Xes. Thus the three symbols form an upward progress, from cross to X.

Ur-Board Symbols ∗ Personal Values

Private

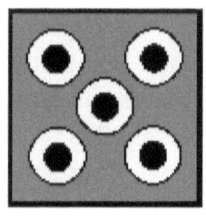

The LIVING

The Closed Gates
of Birth and Death

The DEAD

Community Tradition

Public

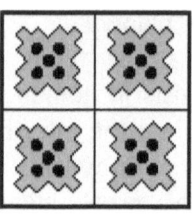

<u>The Gate
of Life</u>

Human Family

Our Common Humanity

The Five
Senses

Individual Experience

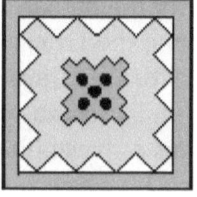

<u>Quarters</u>

Civil Rights

**Equality before God
and under Law**

Fulfillment

Beauty of Character

<u>Stars</u>

Personal
Freedom

Self-Determination

5. The Triads: Synthesis and Progress

These six tile designs form two Triads, one concerning Private life, the other concerning our Public ideals.

In the first Triad, Gates represents a <u>condition</u> of life; Coins is a <u>crisis</u> that takes place in that condition; and Flowers is the desired <u>end,</u> the resolution of the conflict. The story goes like this...

GATES: The condition into which we are born is called Original Sin. We are divided in spirit and imprisoned by our own beliefs. But the Faith of our Fathers provides a safe haven for us in our homes.

COINS: A crisis occurs when the young person leaves home and enters adult life. He develops a will of his own, which may be contrary to the tradition; if he persists in conflict, he either changes his condition or learns to accept it. In either case, the conflict is usually resolved.

FLOWERS: Once the conflict is resolved, the newly empowered person becomes an adult; he or she glows with character, purpose, and determination. This is the Happy Ending symbolized by a Flower.

How do Gates and Coins interact in such a way as to produce Flowers? By the simplest form of synthesis— Addition. The **four** of Gates added to the **five** of Coins, equals the **nine** (8 petals and the center) of Flowers. Thus the theme of the Private Triad is "Synthesis."

That is to say, successful adaptation is a union of the conflicting values of tradition and individual experience.

The theme of the Public Triad is "Progress." This Triad can be described as the three ideals of modern Democracy: Brotherhood, Equality, and Freedom. They arise in separate phases of Private life.

Brotherhood recalls the experiences of childhood, among family and friends. Equality recalls competition in school, and later on in society. The final condition, Freedom, is the mature state, the crown of a person's life, unique for each person.

These are the phases of a progressive life. They fit into a concept of life symbolized by the Ur-board Form. Where that Form comes from is the subject of the next chart and chapter.

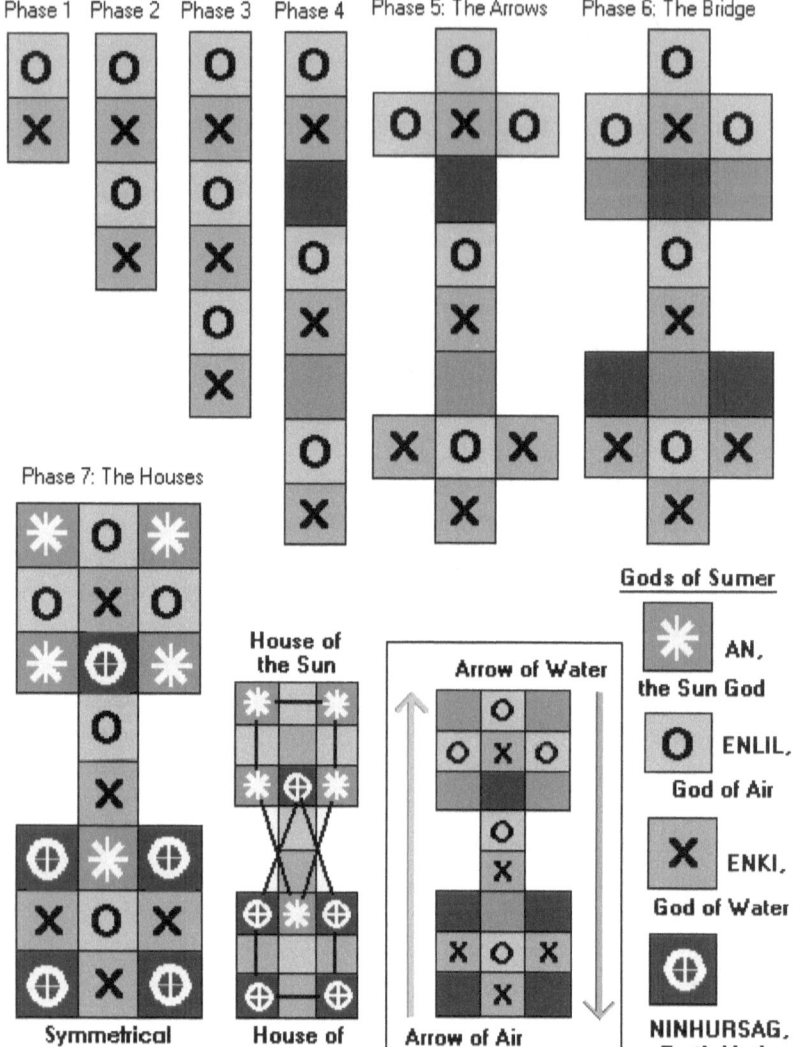

Phase 1 Phase 2 Phase 3 Phase 4 Phase 5: The Arrows Phase 6: The Bridge

Phase 7: The Houses

Symmetrical
Ur-board

House of
the Sun

House of
the Earth

Arrow of Water

Arrow of Air

Gods of Sumer

AN,
the Sun God

ENLIL,
God of Air

ENKI,
God of Water

NINHURSAG,
Earth Mother

6. Origin of the Ur-Board: First Seven Phases

The Ur-board originates **(Phase 1)** with two tiles, an O and an X. The open form of the O makes it an apt symbol of Air (the vacuous firmament), and the X stands for the critical depths below the air, the primal Waters of Life. Thus, Air over Water, yellow over green, O over X.

Increasing complexity gives rise to a slightly more complicated game, requiring a new board **(Phase 2)** with four squares (one O-X above another O-X) for a game using two dice and two markers.

The success of that move prompts us to try three pairs **(Phase 3)**, using three dice and three markers. But such a board lacks character; it seems to be merely a string of Os and Xs.

So we introduce squares to divide the three pairs, a blue tile above the middle pair, and a red tile below it, in a game using four dice and four markers. This long thin game board **(Phase 4)** introduces the central shaft for all future Ur-boards.

But the red and blue tiles do not solve the problem of the Ur-board's Borders: the two ends look alike. So we take the unusual step of adding "sidecars" around the opponent's tile at either end. This is the first use of "5-tile suits," with their distinctive symbolic designs; like these, which made this game board **(Phase 5)** a symbol of dynamic equilibrium between the elements of Air and Water.

So far, all attention has been focused on the ends, leaving the middle empty and uninteresting. So we add red and blue tiles to the sides, making the "bridge crossing" in the middle hazardous for aggressors. Hence, the **(Phase 6)** board, with six dice and six markers.

But now, we have four suits— two suits with *five* tiles, and two suits with *three*? Why not just have four suits of five? We try it— and suddenly **the Ur-board lights up!** The reds and blues of the **Phase 7** board assume symbolic forms of their own, and come to dominate the board.

This is the "symmetrical Ur-board," a 20-tile game board with 4 suits of 5. It is not yet the Sumerian Ur-board, but at this point it is already a complete symbol. It symbolizes the world view of the Sumerians, with the House of the Sun looming above the House of Earth; while the Arrows of O and X show the Air rising and Water falling, in the unending cycle of evaporation and precipitation that has nourished life on earth. And the four suits of the Ur-board correspond to the old gods of Sumer.

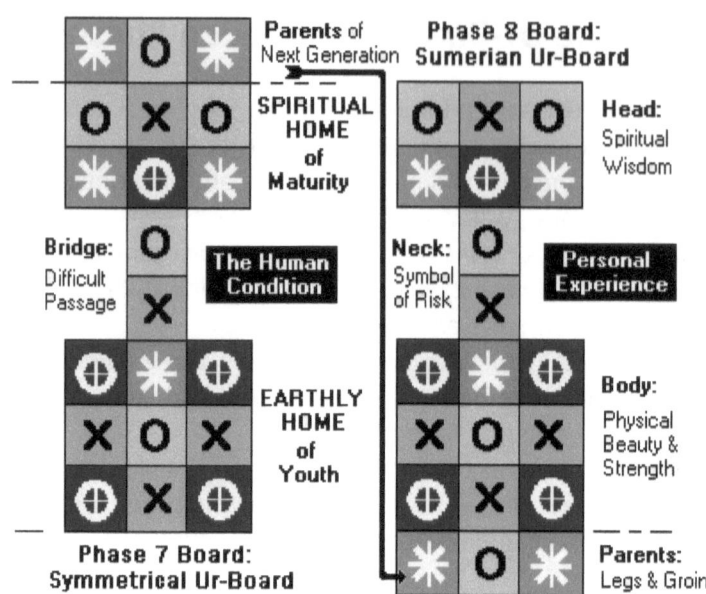

Phase 8 Board: Sumerian Ur-Board

Parents of Next Generation

SPIRITUAL HOME of Maturity

Head: Spiritual Wisdom

Bridge: Difficult Passage

The Human Condition

Neck: Symbol of Risk

Personal Experience

EARTHLY HOME of Youth

Body: Physical Beauty & Strength

Phase 7 Board: Symmetrical Ur-Board

Parents: Legs & Groin

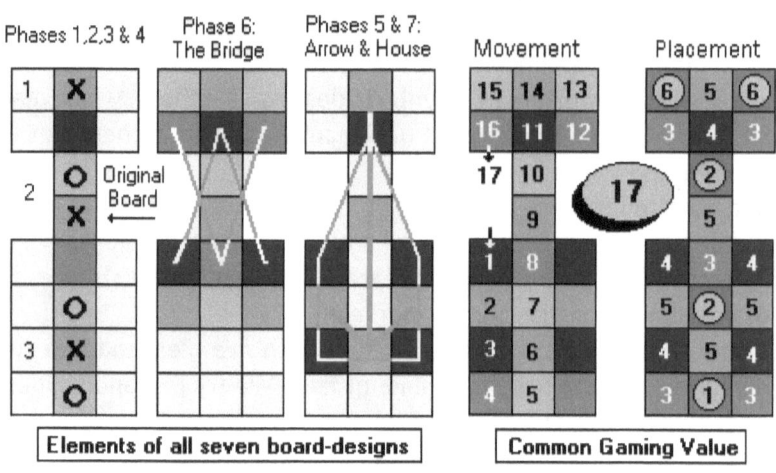

Phases 1,2,3 & 4

Phase 6: The Bridge

Phases 5 & 7: Arrow & House

Original Board

Movement

Placement

15	14	13
16	11	12
17	10	
	9	
1	8	
2	7	
3	6	
4	5	

17

6	5	6
3	4	3
	2	
	5	
4	3	4
5	2	5
4	5	4
3	1	3

Elements of all seven board-designs

Common Gaming Value

7. Origin of the Ur-Board: The Phase 8 Board

The Phase 7 Ur-board, as we imagined it, would no doubt have been a source of pride and satisfaction for the priests of Ur. It was beautiful and "meaningful," *profoundly* meaningful— a symbol of Sumerian religion!

But there were problems with the board. As a game board, it was limited by its rigorous symmetry to one or two simple games. And as a symbol, though it represented the human condition and the passage through life, it also rose up to symbolize Heaven and Earth in Sumerian cosmology— and therein lay its tragic flaw. For when you stand the symmetrical Ur-board upright, its top seems about to topple, its neck about to snap, and the whole figure about to collapse like the tower of Babel. It was painful to look at. People were rioting in the streets.

We can imagine the consternation in the Temple bureaucracy.

But then one day a stranger rode into town (some say it was Lord Enki in disguise) who resolved the dilemma to everyone's satisfaction. By removing the top line of the Phase 7 board and placing it at the bottom of the board (implying the cycle of generation, as the parents assume the role of nature of a person's life), he created the **Phase 8** board, a vertical figure that was poised like a standing person. He had broken symmetry— but only to create a new symmetry in the giant X of An-stars. And the new design featured elements of all the previous boards. Most importantly, the Original (2-tile) Board (with O over X) was prominently displayed in the neck. Then there were remnants of all the other boards, including an Arrow and a House, so that the new Ur-board was a synthesis of all its predecessors.

And it was a much more versatile design. Already we can see two new patterns of play (bottom right), one for *movement* around the board, and one for the *placement* of numbers on the board, united by the number 17. For movement around the board ends with the 17th move, when the marker jumps off; and as for placement— the numbers of the Rooms suit (1, 2, 2, 6, and 6)— add up to 17.

But where did those Rooms suit numbers come from?

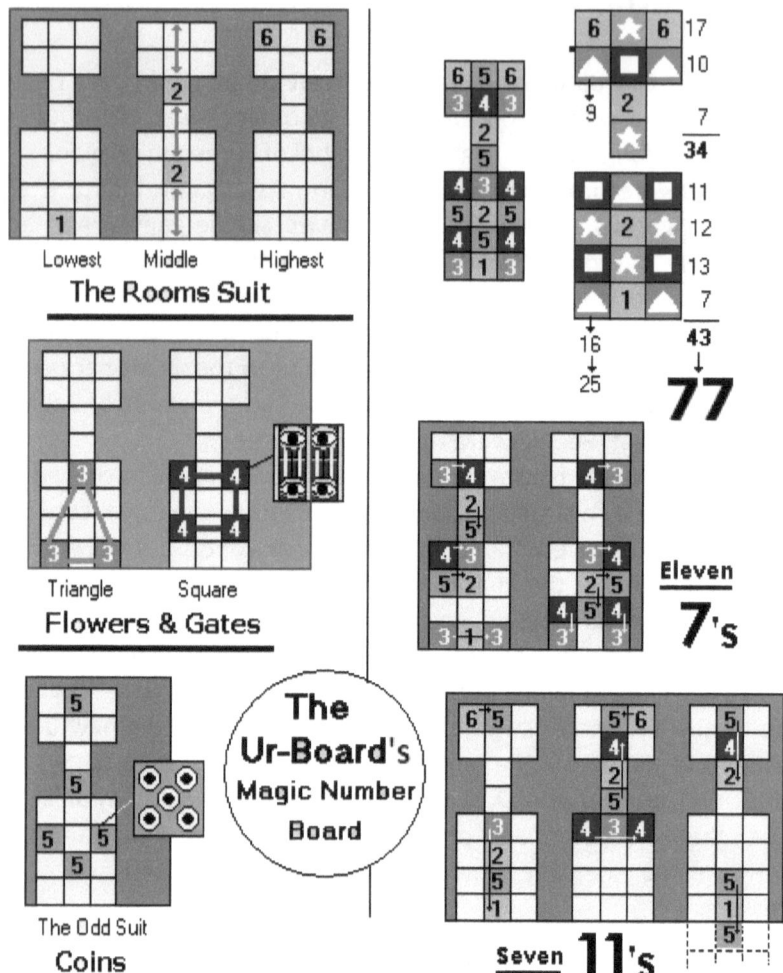

The Rooms Suit

Lowest — Middle — Highest

Flowers & Gates

Triangle — Square

Coins

The Odd Suit

The Ur-Board's Magic Number Board

Eleven 7's

Seven 11's

8. The Magic Number Board

In order to create a placement game in which you roll to place markers on the Ur-Board, you must divide the twenty tiles into six groups, one for each number on a die. Well, there are six tile designs in the Sumerian Ur-board, three of which are in the yellow suit. The bottom tile of that suit should be the 1, for there is only one of that design. The two in the center aisle should be 2, not only because there are two of them, but also because there are two spaces between them, and two between each and its end of the board— in effect defining the middle of the board. And if the bottom inside tile is the lowest number (1), the top outside tiles should be the highest (6).

The red and blue suits are numbered by the figures they form in the body of the board, a *triangle* and *square,* 3 and 4 respectively. And the remaining green suit gets the remaining number, 5. (There seems to be no reason why it should be a 5, but the designers of the tile symbols left no doubt that 5 is the number it would be.)

The resulting board design has some curious features. The side numbers, for instance. In the head they add up to 9; in the body, 16; and together, 25; which reproduces the familiar Pythagorean equation, $3^2+4^2=5^2$. Also, the eight tiles of the center shaft add up to 27 (3^3), as do the six tiles in the head.

But even more impressive is the Ur-board's tribute to the game of craps, with its winning numbers, 7 and 11. For the top half of the board totals 34, and the bottom half 43, for an overall total of 77 (7x11). The neck tiles equal 7, the bottom line has a triplet that equals 7, and the top line has two pairs that equal 11. And there are eleven 7's on the Number Board, and (counting the one made by stacking the board) seven 11's.

Seven and eleven have defined the Ur-board, but seventeen sets the seal on it. You may recall that the number seventeen united the two types of games that were made possible by the Phase 8 Board: the movement game and the placement game. Now the number 17, sensing our momentary doubt, steps in and offers to demonstrate its approval of the Number Board design. And so we take a moment to reveal what the number seventeen might have meant in the sacred numerology of the Ur-board.

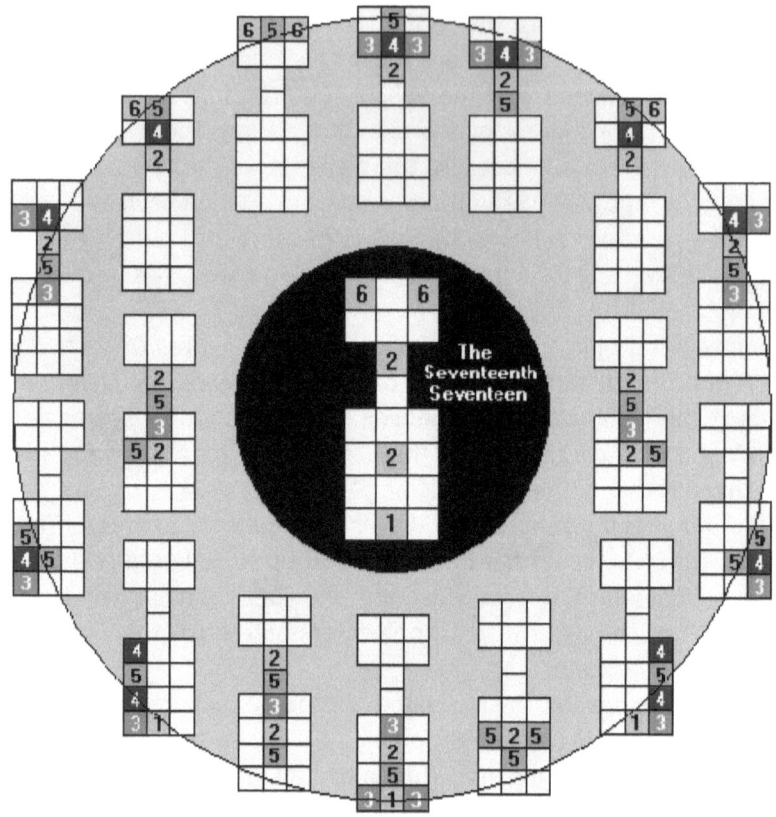

The Eye of God

9. The Seal of Approval

I do not know what the number seventeen meant to the Magi of Ur. But, you see, the priests of Ur were keepers of secret mystical doctrines, which inspired people throughout the Mediterranean for many centuries. Their influence spread westward to Egypt and Crete, and northward to Syria, through Lydia and the Aegean, to the Etruscans of northern Italy, who practiced priestly divination among the Romans. All those who fell under the spell of the Chaldean mysteries became famous for their wisdom. What that wisdom was we do not know, but it involved elements of all the mystical disciplines— such as the proper alignment of homes and temples, astrological computation, the reading of bird entrails, and numerology. Especially numerology.

So, I propose that the prime number 17 occupied a position of some prominence in the numerological system of Sumer. Because, only then can we comprehend the decision of the high priests of Ur to drop the Symmetrical (Phase 7) Ur-Board and adopt the new Unsymmetrical (Phase 8) Ur-Board, simply because 17 was involved in the decision. The number 17 was revered as the number of the Chase Path, because it was thought to be the God-ordained order of things. But when they found out that the O suit (the yellow Rooms suit) which had been fractured and distributed unevenly on the board, contained a series of three numbers— a one, two 2's, and two 6's— which also equal 17, they were astonished and impressed; for a while, and then... not so much. But the stranger (Lord Enki) who had introduced the Phase 8 board noticed their indifference, and asked if he might demonstrate *His* response, using the Magic Number Board. And He opened before them his great cosmic Eye, and cast a rainbow of 16 Ur-Boards, each with the sum of 17 in its design; and the Rooms suit was enshrined in the pupil of God, as the Seventeenth Seventeen, the signature of the Creator!

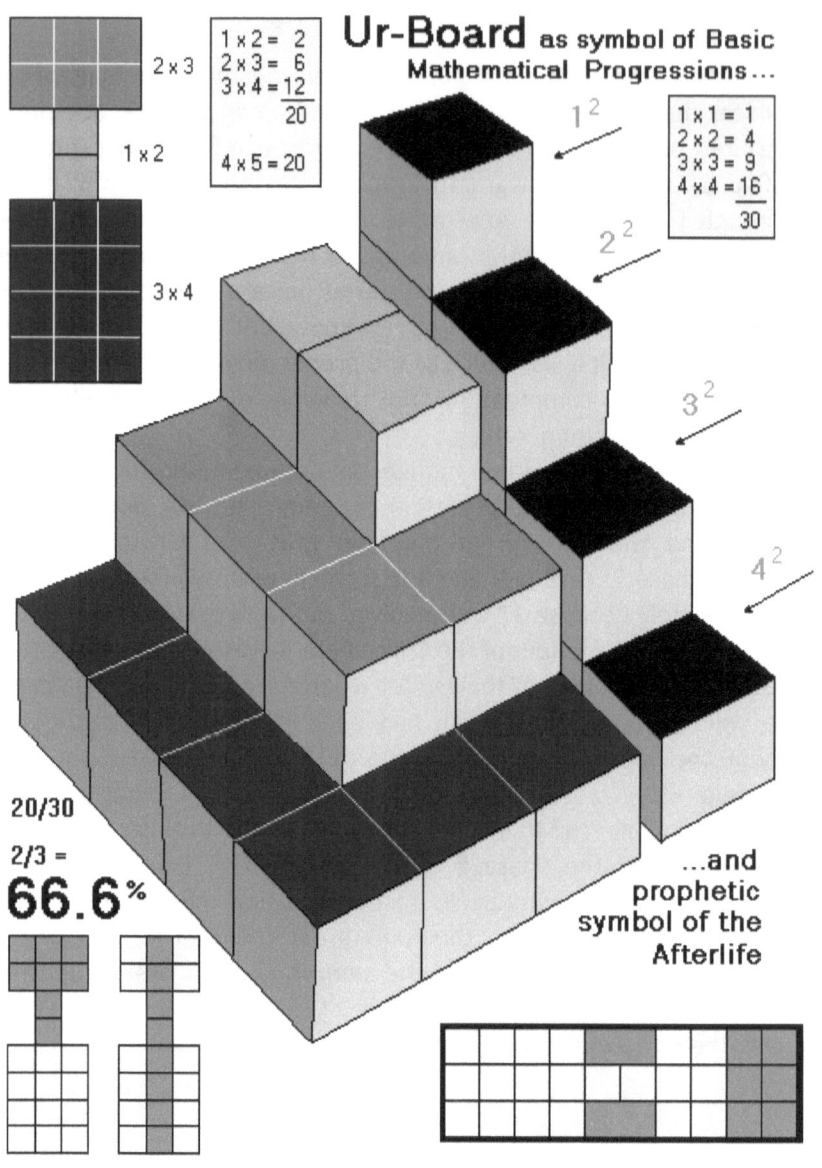

2 x 3

1 x 2

3 x 4

$$1 \times 2 = 2$$
$$2 \times 3 = 6$$
$$3 \times 4 = \underline{12}$$
$$\underline{20}$$

$$4 \times 5 = 20$$

Ur-Board as symbol of Basic
Mathematical Progressions...

1^2

2^2

3^2

4^2

$$1 \times 1 = 1$$
$$2 \times 2 = 4$$
$$3 \times 3 = 9$$
$$4 \times 4 = \underline{16}$$
$$\underline{30}$$

20/30

2/3 =
66.6%

...and
prophetic
symbol of the
Afterlife

10. The Two-thirds Ratio

The Sumerian Ur-board evolved from such simple circumstances, mathematically, that it embodies many basic progressions. The neck, head, and body, for instance, comprise the most basic rectangular proportions— 1 x 2, 2 x 3, and 3 x 4— which together equals the sum of 4 x 5. And thus a figure in 3 parts (with 2, 6, and 12 tiles) can equal 4 suits of 5 symbols, for both equal 20 (2+6+12 = 4x5 = 20).

But, when we render the tiles as 3-dimensional squares (or cubes), they stand one atop the other, so that the stacked part is always one half the number of the unstacked blocks, maintaining a two-thirds relationship between them.

If we add a stairway of ten blocks to the back of that figure, concluding at the top with a single block (which in effect adds a line to each layer, making it square) the resulting figure (as indicated in the illustration) would be a Pyramid of blocks, containing the progression— 1^2, 2^2, 3^2, and 4^2— which equals thirty. The Ur-board is, therefore, an incomplete figure, two-thirds of a true Pyramid.

You may have noticed the *two-thirds ratio* in the Ur-board form— the 8 tiles in the head, to 12 in the body; and the 8 tiles in the center shaft, to 12 in the side aisles. Eight is to twelve like as twenty is to thirty. So, what is the Ur-board two-thirds of?

The answer is implied by the recumbent Ur-board, lying as in a coffin within a 30-tile field. What it adds to the Ur-board are six dark tiles, forming a sestet above the head, equal in size to the head, so that the head portion becomes as large as the body. These dark tiles take their place in the life-form, as the final phase. There is, in other words, a phase of life beyond death.

The Golden Mean

in the Ur-Board

φ phi

1.6

Ur-Board Measure

"Three is to Five, as Five

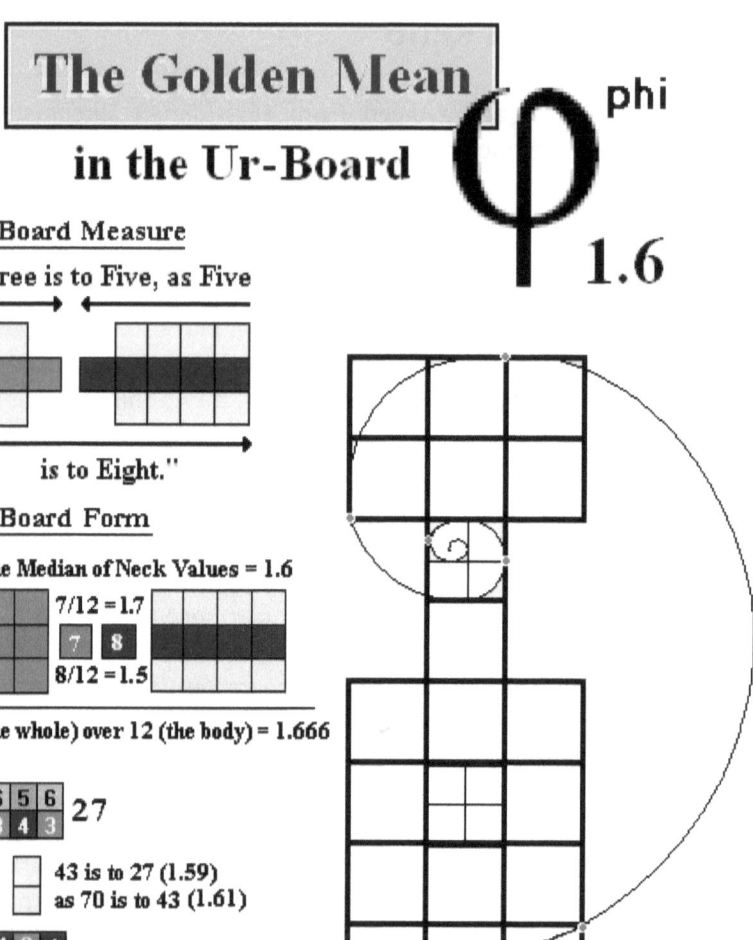

is to Eight."

Ur-Board Form

The Median of Neck Values = 1.6

7/12 = 1.7

7 8

8/12 = 1.5

20 (the whole) over 12 (the body) = 1.666

6	5	6
3	4	3

27

70

43 is to 27 (1.59)
as 70 is to 43 (1.61)

4	3	4
5	2	5
4	5	4
3	1	3

43   Number Board

The Fibonacci Curve

11. The Golden Mean

The Golden Mean is not really a mathematical ratio, but an aesthetic one. Many works of art, especially during the classical Greek period, were based on the Golden Mean, but only the Ur-board set out to measure and explain it. And that, some two thousand years before the classical era!

The Ur-board is a meter stick for the Golden Mean. It contains the most basic formula and the clearest example of the ratio: "Three is to Five, as Five is to Eight." The smaller portion of the line has the same relation to the larger, as the larger portion has to the whole line. When that happens, the ratio is 1.6, the number represented by the Greek letter Phi. Thus, 5/3 (the body divided by the head) is 1.666; then 8/5 (the whole line divided by the body) is exactly 1.6. But the measure doesn't have to be perfect. In fact, Phi (like Pi) is almost always an approximation; so a very near approximation must be regarded as a hit.

What happens when you add the side aisles of the board— that is, when you're working with 20 tiles instead of 8? Does the Ur-board lose its Golden ratio? No, but now you must remove the neck and use it to "fine tune" the ratio. If you keep only the 7th tile, the ratio is 1.7; if you include the 8th tile as well, the ratio is 1.5. So, the Golden ratio (1.6) occurs precisely in the uncharted middle.

Finally, what happens when you add the Magic Numbers? Do the numbers observe the Golden ratio? Yes, they do. But you must remove the neck again. Good. Now the two parts of the Ur-board (head and body) have a ratio of 1.59, and the body and the whole decapitated Ur-board have a ratio of 1.61 (only a .02 difference).

So, the Ur-board remains true to its Ideal of Beauty—as a line, as a figure, and as a numerical construct.

Anything else?

Yes. The Fibonacci curve, based on the series of numbers obtained by adding the previous numbers together (1, 1, 2, 3, 5, 8...)— when it originates in a quarter of a Quarters (Rooms) tile and circles around, expanding until it finally flies off into space— the figure it makes fits the Ur-board so perfectly that it touches upon key lines and corners, and defines the structure of the board.

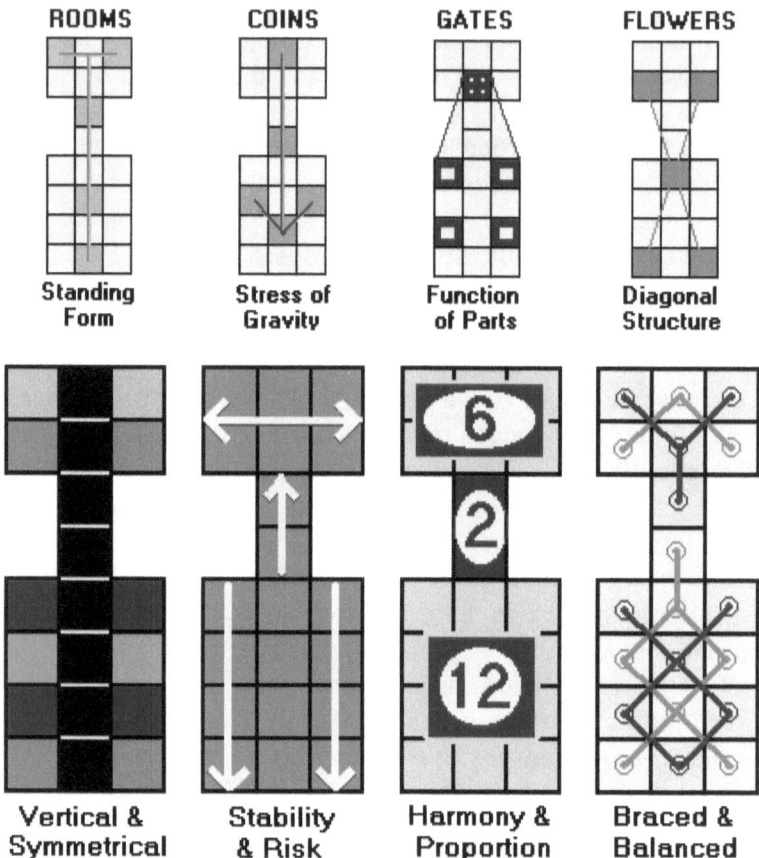

Architectonic Analysis

ROOMS — Standing Form

COINS — Stress of Gravity

GATES — Function of Parts

FLOWERS — Diagonal Structure

Vertical & Symmetrical

Stability & Risk

Harmony & Proportion

6

2

12

Braced & Balanced

12. A Standing Figure

The most impressive evidence of self-conscious design in the Ur-board is the analysis of its own beauty, carried out by the four suits.

Rooms remind us of the Ur-board's mission— to be a *standing figure*. We see the Rooms suit standing precariously on one foot, with its head in the clouds. It's a proud figure, but there's a problem. *The stress of gravity*, says Coins. *Gravity tends to pull down any vertical figure. Yes*, Gates says, nodding. *That's why people make bottom-heavy and short things, that won't topple over. This practice ends in pyramid building. But the pyramid does not stand, it squats.* The others agree. *Maybe*, Flowers suggests, *we can create a balanced design, with legs spread like the sides of a pyramid, and a top to match, only less bulky, with perhaps a diagonal structure to hold it up.*

The Ur-board overhears this conversation, and says, "Don't worry, my children, I've taken care of all those problems. You see, Rooms, to be a firm standing figure, I limited my structure to one tall shaft, with sides symmetrically arranged. The sides prevent the shaft from leaning, and keep the figure in balance.

"Observe, Coins, how stable it is. It has a large solid base, upholding a smaller head. The only place gravity threatens is at the neck. *So why is there a neck?* Because a solid vertical slab lacks interest. Like a pyramid, it has no parts. So, halfway up the figure, I decided to generate interest by balancing a horizontal segment (a head) on a vertical stem (a neck). Defying Gravity will hold their interest, I figured.

"And then, Gates, I created a harmonious relationship between the three parts by keeping everything simple— minimal and consistent. For the neck to be vertical, it had to have two unit blocks, one above the other. For the head to be horizontal it had to have a line of three blocks; but one line of three would look fragile, so once again I doubled the lines. And finally, to make the base equal to its task, I doubled the head in the body. By this act of *doubling*, I established a form that expressed its own principle of design in the mathematical formula, 6 x 2 = 12.

"Of course the head still overlaps the neck, so I created an internal checkerboard pattern, to brace the figure: Rooms and Gates are flat, square designs; Coins and Flowers are centered and round. The checkerboard design they create laces the blocks together."

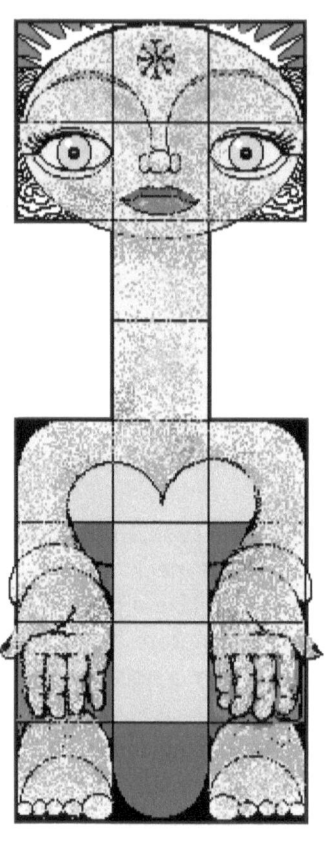

Anthropomorphic Analogy

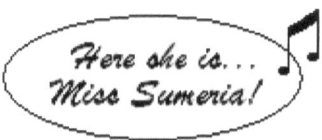

Here she is...
Miss Sumeria!

Crown	Brow	Crown	Self-Determination
Eye	Face	Eye	Conscious Awareness
↓	Throat		Risk
↑	Voice		
Shoulder	Heart	Shoulder	Personal Relationship
Arm	Chest	Arm	Competition
Hand	Gut	Hand	Friendship
Leg	Groin	Leg	Parental Support

The Ur-Board: Symbol of Body Wisdom

13. A Familiar Form

Not only does the Ur-board correspond in its three parts (head, neck, and body) to the human physique, its 20 tiles also correspond to the various parts of the body, with the symmetrical limbs around the abdomen and chest, and the symmetrical sense organs around the face. This design, as a pattern of human life, begins in childhood, at the bottom, and proceeds upward toward maturity.

When dealing with the Ur-board form, we always begin at the bottom and read our way up the board, rather than from the top down. This is in keeping with Nature, wherein things grow up from ground level and reach toward the Sun, symbolizing progress. Just so, the pattern of change from one quarter of the board to the next is progressive, from physical security and enjoyment in the bottom quarter, to ideals of personal achievement and affection in the upper torso; and from self-definition in the neck, to spiritual union with the world in the head. This upward progress corresponds to that which takes place in life.

The interpretations of the various parts of the body are derived from common sense. Hence, the legs (like columns that support the body) stand for the parents; the space between them, called the Gate of Life, symbolizes the womb, or the home of childhood. The hands we hold and shake are signs of friendship, which is love at the gut level. The gut, or belly, is a symbol of appetite and pleasure. Above the gut is the chest, symbol of prowess in battle; it is surrounded by arms. Above the chest is the breast, symbol of tenderness in love; it is surrounded by the shoulders of responsibility. The neck is divided by its two functions, to take in and to give out, as in breathing. This union of opposite movements through the same passage is risky, as are all things related to the neck. In the head, the eyes are symbols of awareness, and the face is the central symbol of one's identity. Above the face, the brow (or third eye) symbolizes the ultimate in human wisdom, and the crowning brain, the ultimate in independent judgment and self-rule.

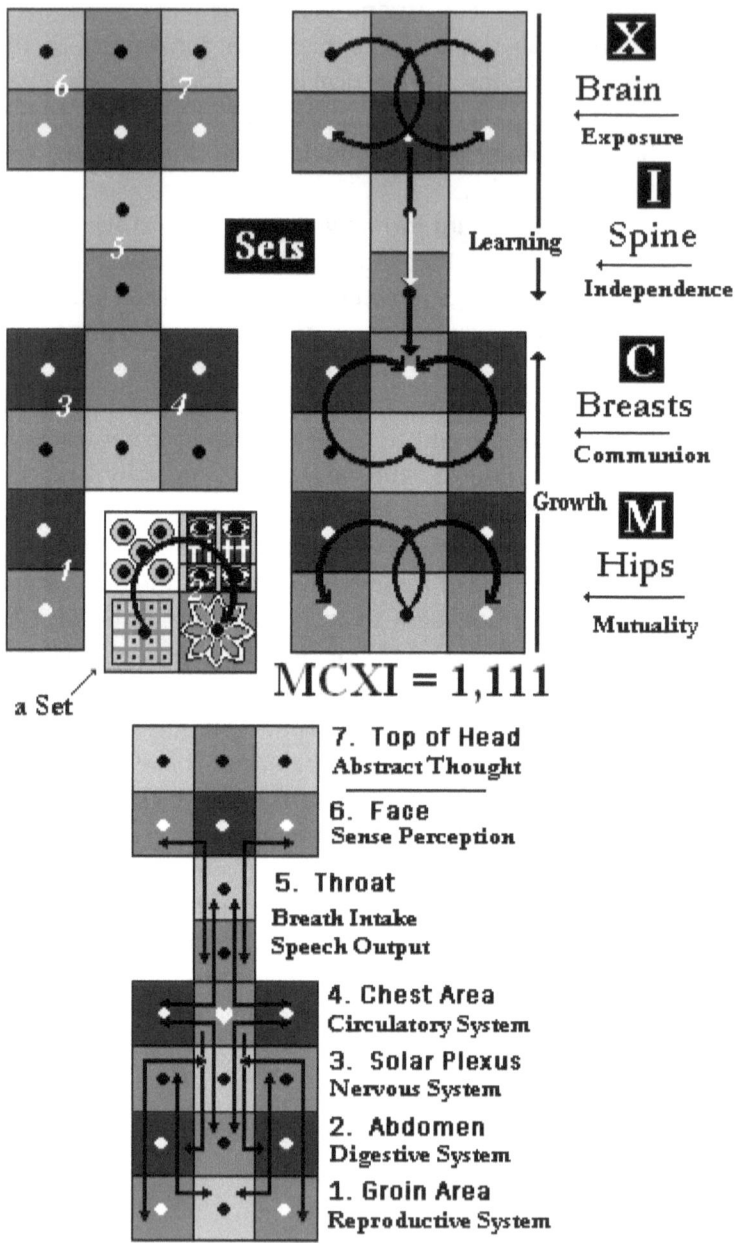

Sets

X Brain
← Exposure

I Spine
← Learning
Independence

C Breasts
← Communion

Growth **M** Hips
← Mutuality

a Set

MCXI = 1,111

7. **Top of Head**
Abstract Thought

6. **Face**
Sense Perception

5. **Throat**
Breath Intake
Speech Output

4. **Chest Area**
Circulatory System

3. **Solar Plexus**
Nervous System

2. **Abdomen**
Digestive System

1. **Groin Area**
Reproductive System

14. Bodily Organs and Systems

As you scan the Ur-board's structure, you may observe that each corner of the board has a block of four tiles, containing all four colors—these are called "sets." There are four sets in the body section, two sets in the head, and one set strung out in the neck, for a total of seven.

The bottom sets determine the canonical order in which the suits are arranged— Rooms, Coins, Gates, and Flowers (yellow, green, blue, and red). We enter at the Gate of Life (yellow), and proceed upward to Coins (green); but then, since the next line repeats those two suits, we must turn aside to Gates (blue) and drop down to Flowers (red). The resulting motion is circular, on both sides. The same order of movement in the upper torso and head also results in circular motions, but in two different directions. And in the neck, that order of movement points downward from the head.

Thus, we encounter a force in the Ur-board known only to pool sharks and nuclear physicists— "spin." In the bottom arcs, the spin shows the form of female hips, working in unison to move and support a standing figure; the middle arcs form breasts, or ribs, open to each other but closed to the world; the line in the neck indicates the flexible structure of the spine, and the flow of nervous impulses carrying messages from the head; and the topmost arcs symbolize the exposed sense organs of the head, open to the world. The point of this analysis is the logic of the body's structure: the base of the body is a bone mechanism, to keep the body balanced as it moves about; the chest cavity is a bone encasement to hold the delicate organs together, and keep them safe; the neck provides a mobile stand for the head, and a duct for food, water, and air to pass into the body; and only then, at the height of the body, does it open the portholes of perception to the outer world.

There are also a dozen L's in the Ur-board's structure (L-shaped figures, consisting of all four colors). They might represent the flow of energy (Chee) throughout the body, as envisioned by Asian medicine men. This schematic would serve as circuitry for the seven functions indicated (to the right of the board) for the six lines and the neck, all of which remind us of the seven Chakras, or "gateways to the soul."

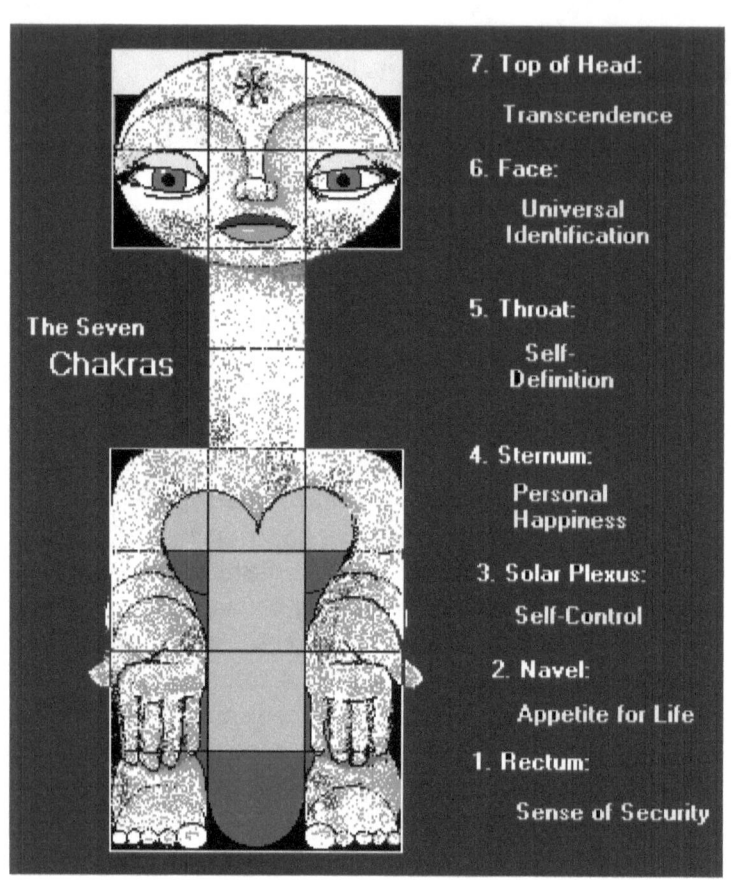

The Seven
Chakras

7. Top of Head:
  Transcendence

6. Face:
  Universal
  Identification

5. Throat:
  Self-
  Definition

4. Sternum:
  Personal
  Happiness

3. Solar Plexus:
  Self-Control

2. Navel:
  Appetite for Life

1. Rectum:
  Sense of Security

Asiatic Analogy

15. Ancient Chakras

Now that the Ur-board has an anatomy, we can point directly to the vital centers of the body, and see how they are symbolized. They begin at the bottom, where Fear and Appetite dwell. They emerge in puberty as contentious Valor and complacent Satisfaction. And having slipped through the narrow defile of Public life, they arise and know themselves at last, as dying animals.

Or: they begin with Confidence and Enthusiasm in childhood, and emerge in young adulthood as disciplined Truth and sympathetic Love. And having worked to improve the Public condition, they arise and know themselves at last, as immortal spirits.

The Hindu chakras are in general agreement with the older Ur-board. They locate the Base Chakra, precisely, in the brief space between the genitals and rectum. The Ur-board doesn't specify that closely; it just points to the groin area. I called it the Rectum because that's where insecurity registers.

The second chakra is located in the sacrum and linked with the gonads; the Ur-board centers it in the navel. Both places are sources of enthusiasm, creativity, joy, and pleasure; but they are linked with different processes. The Ur-board favors the innocent pleasures of food; the Hindu favors the guilt-ridden pleasures of sex. Since the Ur-board is based on the Life-form, this chakra opens in childhood, before sex is an issue.

The remaining chakras are virtually identical with the remaining lines of the Ur-board. The third eye An-star is placed in the seventh line, rather than the sixth, where it belongs. It signifies the transcendent qualities of the spirit that shine so resplendently in the face.

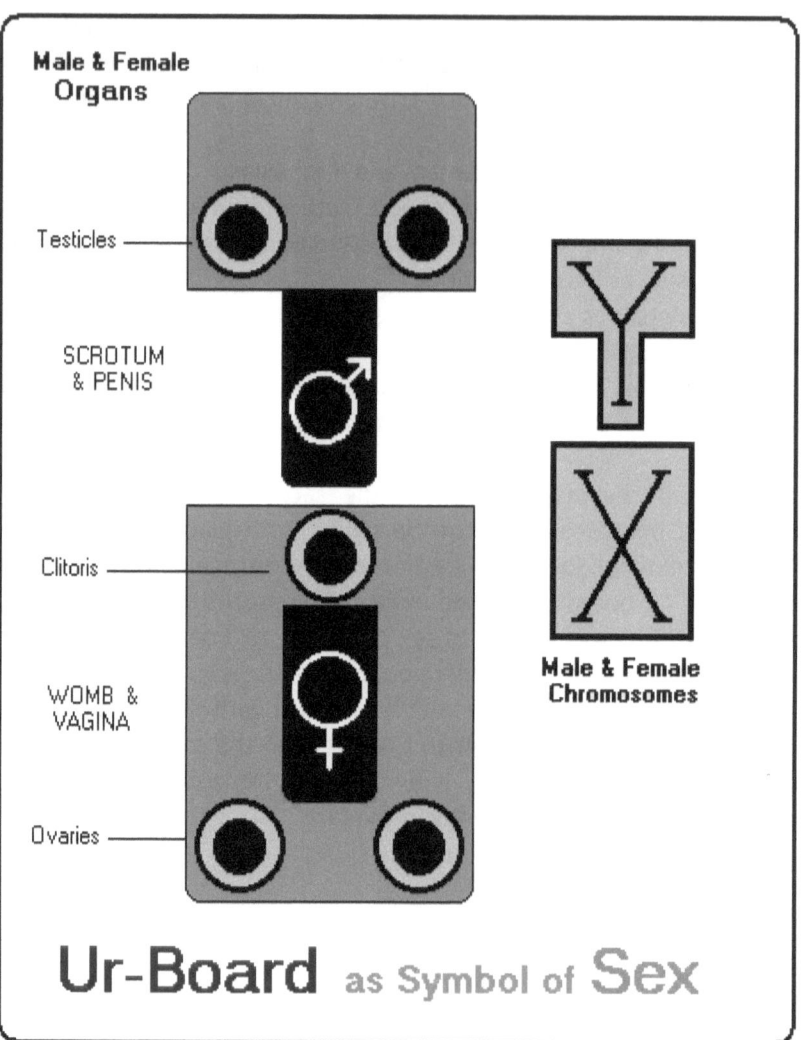

Male & Female Organs

Testicles

SCROTUM & PENIS

Clitoris

WOMB & VAGINA

Ovaries

Male & Female Chromosomes

Ur-Board as Symbol of Sex

16. The Sex Symbol

Once it is pointed out to you, you can't miss the sex symbolism of the Ur-board. What we have been calling the *head* and *neck* are actually an image of the male sex-organs, and the *body* below it symbolizes the female sex-organs. The central elements of the organs (phallus and uterus, in black) are composed of identical tiles: the Quarters tile of the Rooms suit (symbol of competitive activity), and the Coins tile (symbol of worldly knowledge), the mature virtues gained from the experience of sex.

The Flowers represent the organs responsible for the sex-life— the four gonads and the central stimulator, the clitoris. These draw the dark member down until it fills the empty space at the heart of her body, and the testes take their place within the realm of the ovaries.

Even the blank spaces in this design are meaningful— the woman's thighs, which enclose and open to receive, and the man's back, which is exposed and thrusts to enter. They represent the biological specialization of the sexes, and what it teaches us.

The sexual differentiation of the human species instructs us in the duality of our nature: that we live in two spheres, the Private and the Public. The Private sphere is the setting for female values: it originates in the parental home, expands to the school and the local community, and concludes with the creation of a complete person, ready to enter the world. The Public sphere is the setting for male values— the scene of work and competition, which originates in the free, open life-style of the city, and concludes with responsible and self-determining commitments to the future.

The meaning is not that the Private sector is for women and the Public sector for men, although that is a primitive reading of the design. But for moderns it is that the Private sphere (the town or village) "encloses" its members, nourishing and protecting them; whereas the Public sphere (the city) "exposes" its members to risk and scrutiny. The Ur-board is thus proposing a re-structuring of human society into two settings, the towns or villages of regional territories, with their local laws and customs, and Urban Culture in the great cities of the world, where people compete for wealth and power.

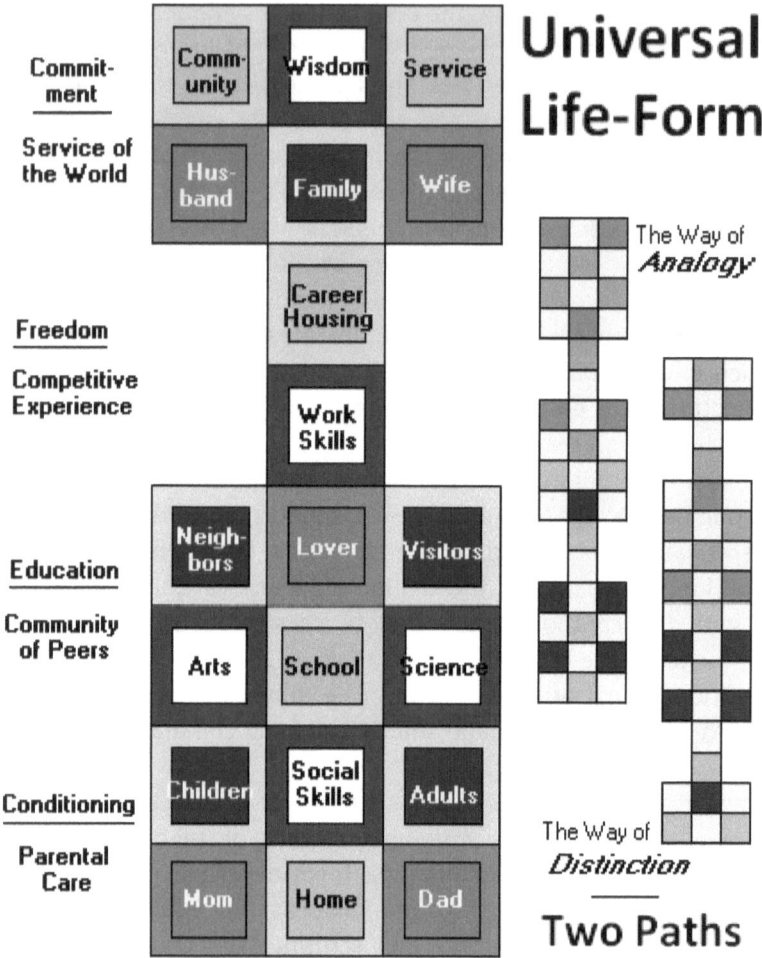

Universal Life-Form

Comm-unity	Wisdom	Service
Hus-band	Family	Wife
	Career Housing	
	Work Skills	
Neigh-bors	Lover	Visitors
Arts	School	Science
Children	Social Skills	Adults
Mom	Home	Dad

Commit-ment

Service of the World

Freedom

Competitive Experience

Education

Community of Peers

Conditioning

Parental Care

The Way of *Analogy*

The Way of *Distinction*
_____

Two Paths

17. The Universal Life-form

The Ur-board presents us with its version of the Human Life-form. There are four phases of active life: Childhood, Adolescence, Adulthood, and Maturity. The four suits represent four concerns within each phase of a person's life: ROOMS (Yellow) Living Quarters; COINS (Green) Learning Conditions; GATES (Blue) Community Relations; and FLOWERS (Red) Personal Attachments.

Life begins at Home, with life-long attachments to Mom and Dad. Outside the home, one lives among friends and neighbors, developing the social skills one will need to live independently at school. For in the future, when a person leaves home, school will be his or her residence from then on, until, as young adults, they decide to get a job and support themselves. In school they will be living with peers, adapting to their generation. And they will be learning about foreign lands, in preparation for a life of travel and work.

When they leave school, they will live in bachelor housing or married apartments, in the town or city where they work. No families with children will be allowed in cities, except as visitors or tourists. Couples will be free to live together, but cannot have families there.

They can work in the city as long as they want to, and retire in midlife to a small town and serve the local community with the skill and experience they gained in the city.

For such a people, Freedom will mean, not merely a state of mind, but a phase of life as well. Freedom is the life-style of young adults. They come from a condition of *dependency;* they will later move into a condition of *responsibility;* but during their work life— in university programs, in working careers or in positions of leadership— they will be free to live with whom they will, and come and go as they please.

In terms of the Life-form, everyone travels the same path in life, to widely different ends. However, in a more complex representation of the Life-form (the double Ur-boards) we see a real difference between paths—the Way of Analogy and the Way of Distinction. Some precocious and promising students will enter competitive life early and remain in the struggle for leadership until late in life; whereas most people will predictably choose to move from phase to phase, as is customary and convenient.

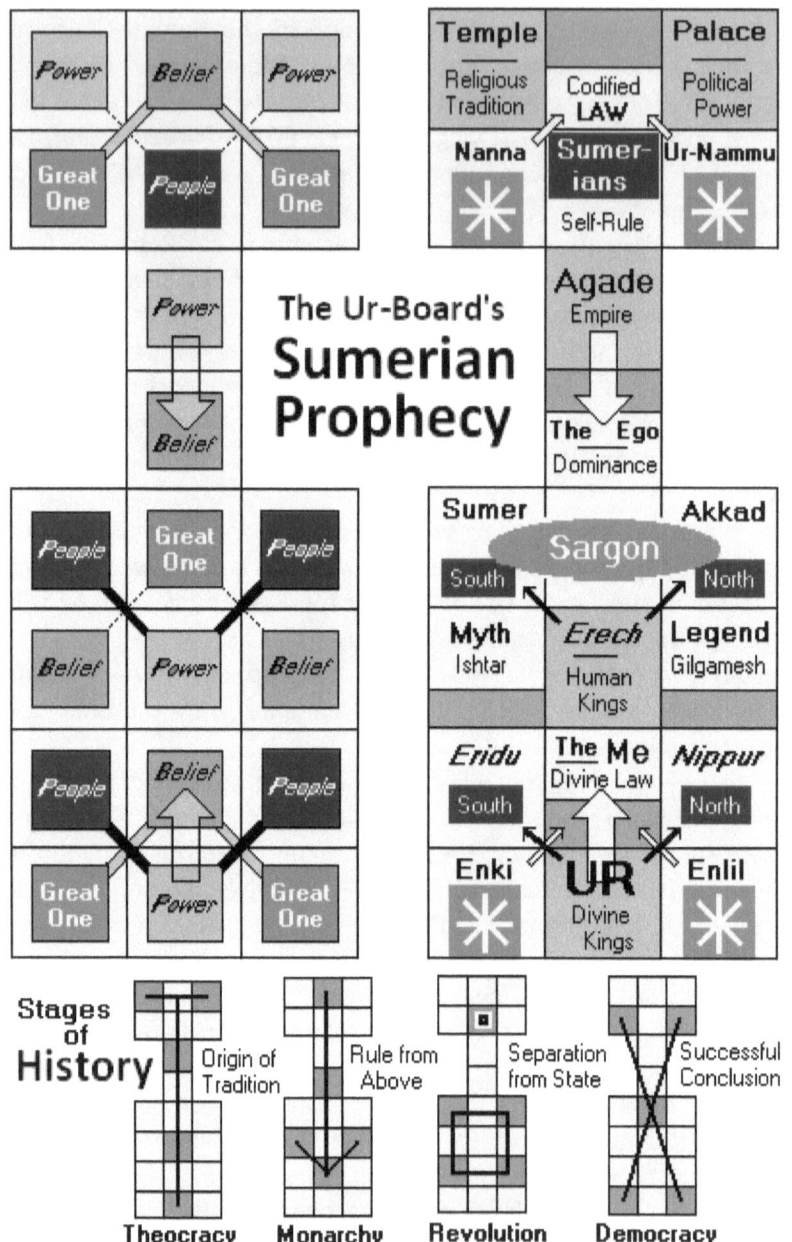

The Ur-Board's
Sumerian Prophecy

Temple		Palace
Religious Tradition	Codified **LAW**	Political Power
Nanna ✳	**Sumer-ians** Self-Rule	**Ur-Nammu** ✳

Agade Empire

The Ego Dominance

Sumer	Sargon	Akkad
South		North
Myth Ishtar	*Erech* Human Kings	**Legend** Gilgamesh
Eridu South	**The Me** Divine Law	*Nippur* North
Enki ✳	**UR** Divine Kings	**Enlil** ✳

Stages of History

Origin of Tradition — **Theocracy**

Rule from Above — **Monarchy**

Separation from State — **Revolution**

Successful Conclusion — **Democracy**

18. Stages of History

The Ur-board symbolizes the structure of Historical change; but that interpretation is not derived from any external analogy, but from the internal logic of its design.

Each suit symbolizes an aspect of institutional history— Power (Rooms) and Belief (Coins), the People (Gates) and the Great Ones (Flowers). The question posed by the structure of the board is: How do the three upper quarters vary from the bottom quarter of the board?

1. In the first phase, notice, the Great Ones create a new Belief, and the ruling Power of the government establishes that Belief and unifies the People. This (according to the Rooms suit design) is the origin of Tradition, in the establishment of a Theocracy.

2. In the second phase, the government still unifies the People, but now the Belief system is not the one created by the Founders, but an analogous faith in the Power of the state, one that inspires devotion to the ruler— a monarch, who rules from above, in imitation of God.

3. In the third phase, the excesses of autocratic rule cause the people to realize that the original condition of the state has been reversed; that the Power to govern no longer arises from their common faith, but is the prerogative of the ruling class to impose its will upon others. The result is the separation of the Great and the Good, and hence the loss of greatness and goodness in the state.

4. In the fourth phase, the revolution comes to a successful, ironic conclusion (according to the Flowers suit design) with the establishment of democratic conditions in the state.

This four phase process had taken place in Sumer, with the rise and fall of Sargon's empire, fulfilling the ancient prophecy of the Ur-board. For as we see in the prophetic Ur-board, in the First Dynasty of Ur the gods Enki and Enlil gave "the Me" (divine law) to the Sumerians; and the kings of Ur established temple rule and unified Sumer— from Eridu in the south, to Nippur in the north. Later the dynasties of Erech established a tradition of strong, defiant rulers (Nimrod, Gilgamesh), which resulted in the reign of Sargon, the prototype of conquerors. After the collapse of his empire and the destruction of his capital, Agade, the Sumerians recovered their sovereignty, and Ur-Nammu the Great, inspired by the patron god of Ur (the moon god, Nanna), oversaw the codification of Law, as the basis of civil life.

UR-BOARD PHILOSOPHY

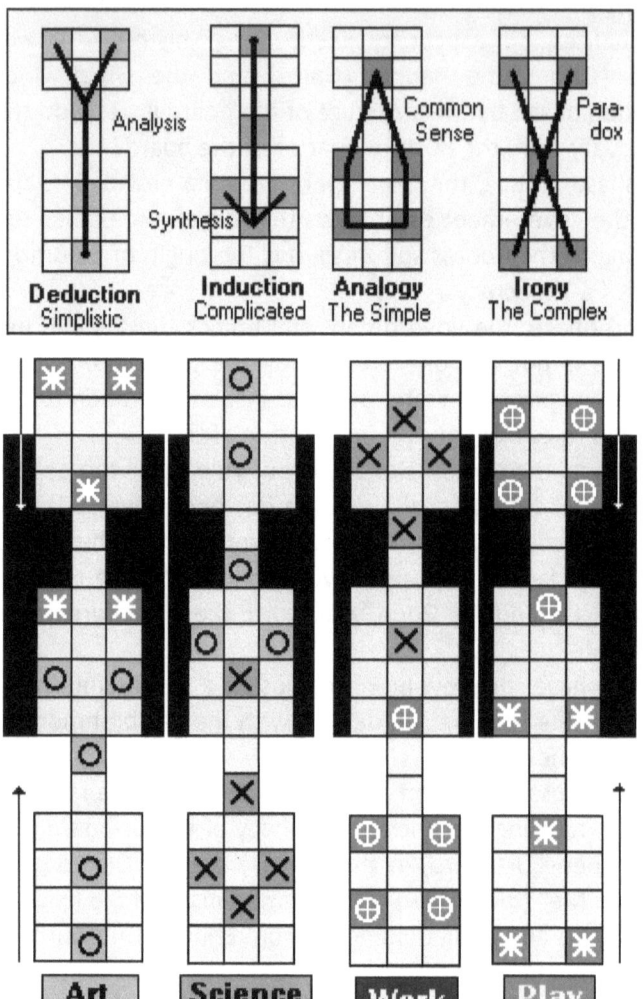

Deduction	**Induction**	**Analogy**	**Irony**
Simplistic	Complicated	The Simple	The Complex

Analysis

Synthesis

Common Sense

Para-dox

Art   Science   Work   Play

19.   States of Mind

Having dealt with *Life* and *History,* the Ur-board now turns its attention to *Thought.*

The dimension of Thought is known to the mind (rational consciousness) through the medium of Public communication, where the mind affirms or reacts to the consensus of public opinion, in the Humanities and Sciences. Criticism and peer review constantly correct the tendency of Deduction to be simplistic and Induction to be pointlessly complicated. These are the methods of the rational mind in world culture; and while they create good Art and Science, they don't bring people in their Private lives closer to the dimension of Thought. Many successful artists and scientists are oddly simplistic or complicated in their personal lives.

There must be a more effective means for learning true Simplicity and Complexity. This is the problem that the Ur-board addresses.

Its ideas on this subject are gathered from Forms stacked head to head. In each of the four columns, the bottom Ur-board form represents how a person enters upon a mental activity; the top form symbolizes the demands of Truth, which comes down in an upside-down Ur-board to meet it— and interrupts the bottom board's conclusion with a newly formed Ur-board (in the black area). Thus, a work of Art sets out to make grand distinctions (Rooms) about human nature, but Irony (Flowers) intervenes and transforms its themes into common sense analogies (Gates). Similarly, Science gathers data (Coins), but before it can come to a conclusion (Rooms), the issue has been complicated by more data (Coins). Hence simplistic humanism and complicated science.

According to the Ur-board, people can profit more from Work and Play, to learn the Truth about life. With Work, you set out to do something simple (Gates), but the imposition of new insights (Coins) causes you to make distinctions (Rooms) about what is meaningful in life. With Play, you begin in an ironic spirit (Flowers) to test your skill at historical pursuits (symbolized by games and sports), and in the end, you learn to have an ironic attitude toward those pursuits (Flowers). Hence simple virtues and complex attitudes.

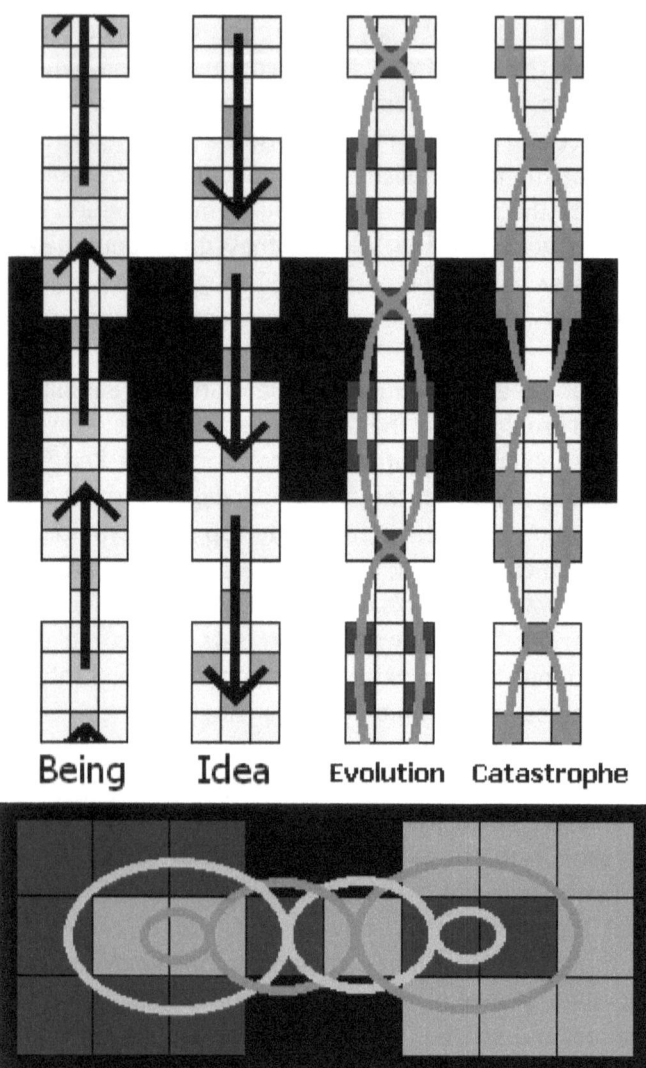

Being   Idea   Evolution   Catastrophe

The Marriage of Heaven and Hell

20. The Loom of Time

We have just seen the Ur-board Form, rising up with the motion of Time, collide with a Form coming down from the end of Time— the collision resulting in the next moment's Form, in the progress of Thought. Where did the idea come from to suggest such a design?

From stacking the forms. When you stack Ur-boards three high, to represent the past, present, and future, you get the idea of Space-Time illustrated by the suits. The Rooms suit, symbolizing Being, rises up out of the Past, heading toward the Future; but at every moment it confronts and must harmonize itself with a flow of Meaning (Coins) emanating from the end of Time. That harmonious adjustment is the Present moment.

The result, as symbolized by the remaining suits (Gates and Flowers), is a cosmic system of two separate interlocking wave-lengths— Creation and Destruction— crossing each other and creating symbols in Time. The two braided waves do not oppose or thwart each other, but act in harmony and shape the world. We see this graphically depicted by the two chains: Gates and Flowers don't fill the space; there is a missing suit between them. But the rhythm caused by this offset arrangement results in the perfect symbolic form of the Scarab.

In this way, galactic masses and atomic nuclei were formed; and thus Evolution and Catastrophe testify to the truth of God, for omnipotent power and divine Intelligence are evident in the forces that cause and govern the evolution of forms.

To the Scientist, Evolution does not imply progress, but only change. But to the Symbolist, all change contributes to the drift of progress, even wars and natural disasters; all things, good and evil, lift us up in Time, toward the perfection of God in Thought. Progress, therefore, is not a human invention, but a natural consequence of the passage of time.

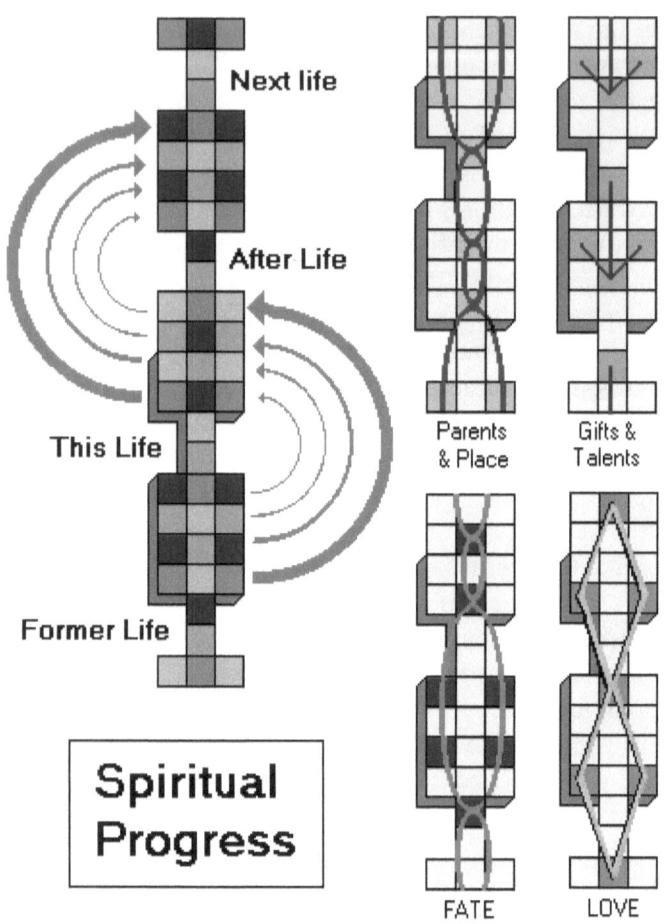

Next life

After Life

This Life

Former Life

Spiritual Progress

Parents & Place

Gifts & Talents

FATE

LOVE

21. The Twist of Fate

However, the human race does add a new twist to the master plan of evolution. Modern Science and Democracy, when they become the unifying principles of history, take up the pursuit of our ultimate destiny and accelerate the rate of Progress. And in death, too (where the soul persists until it is embodied in another person and assumes another identity) the souls of people begin to progress more readily from a life of Sorrow to a life of Joy, by the Modern faith in *personal happiness*.

The soul persists beyond the grave so that each of us may participate, in a self-determining way, in the Progress of human culture. This the soul does, *not* by influencing events on Earth, but by choosing the conditions of its own next life. The soul that frees itself from survival passions (hate, revenge, fear, resentment) will be in Heaven, where it can choose *happiness* as a prime ingredient for the next life. By contrast, a soul in Hell will choose some form of *conflict*, for the sake of pride, revenge, or self-justification.

These are the Ur-board's thoughts, symbolized by a stacking technique implied by the board's vertical symmetry. That is, on a Phase 8 Ur-board (the Sumerian artifact), the line of Gates and Flowers below the neck, and the line of Gates and Flowers above it, are composed of opposite arrangements. That is an obvious pattern. But notice that the lines above and below them are composed of Rooms and Coins in opposite arrangements. Now, there are no lines to contrast with the two bottom lines of the board. If we follow the implication of the Design and create those lines, we see the added lines above the board as a symbol of the soul in the afterlife, where it chooses the conditions of its next life.

The image of the Afterlife is interesting. There you see all in perfect order: the Sun shining down on Earth, with the O and X on either side in the proper order (O over X). The top line is Heaven, where the god within us considers the possibilities for a better life; the bottom line is Hell, where the creature within us plans to avenge his former sufferings and prove himself the master of his fate.

The Ur-board and the Human Genome

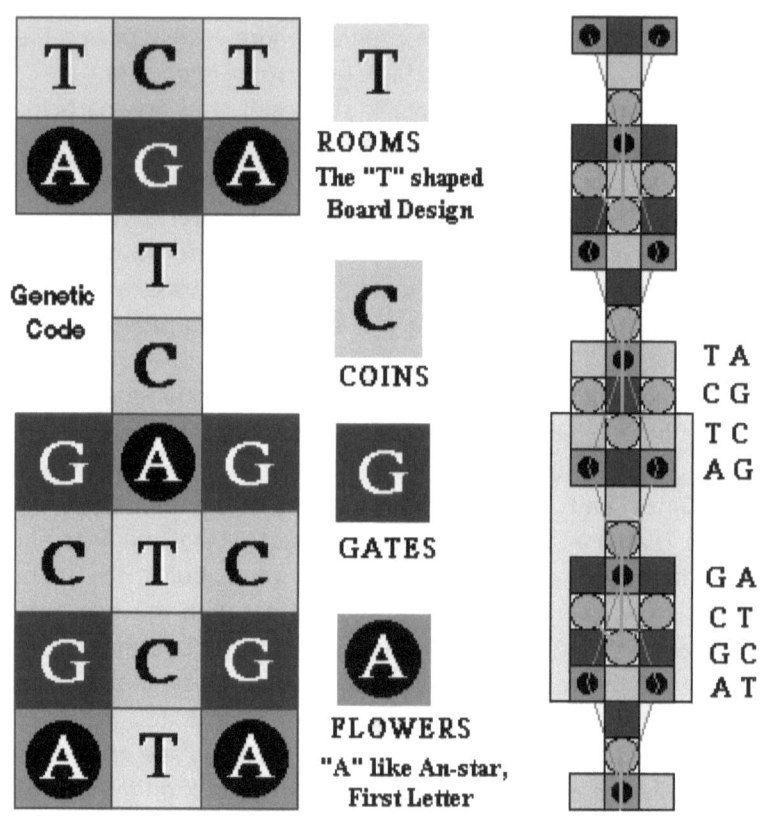

T	C	T
A	G	A
	T	
	C	
G	A	G
C	T	C
G	C	G
A	T	A

Genetic Code

T
ROOMS
The "T" shaped
Board Design

C
COINS

G
GATES

A
FLOWERS
"A" like An-star,
First Letter

T A
C G

T C
A G

G A
C T

G C
A T

22. The Ur-board and the Human Genome

There is every reason to be excited about finding an implied relationship between the Genome and the Ur-board. Because *that* is where it all began: Lord Enki splicing the genes and creating Mankind. And it was the same Lord Enki who much later would give Mankind the Ur-board. The mind boggles considering it. Could the Serpent who gave us Wisdom be sending us the genetic formula for, say, Immortality?

I don't know.

There may be a message of that type, a prophecy meant to be passed on from one king or high priest of Ur to the next, until the day would came when it could be understood. Where would that take place? Well, not in Sumer; not in Babylonia; not in the Persian empire; not in the Pagan empires of Greece or Rome; neither in seats of Christendom nor of Islam; but in another hemisphere and thousands of Earth years later; when mankind had begun to catch up with the science of the Anunnaki; when an offspring of Adam might come upon the ancient game board and find in it intimations of the newly discovered human genome.

No one on Earth planned it that way, yet the timing seems perfect. It seems now to have been the work of Fate— that the city of Ur should be cut off in its prime and buried in toxic waste, that thus the gods' prophetic message (the Ur-board) would lay undisturbed in its chosen grave throughout the slow-moving millennia, to be exhumed just in time that the archeologists who discovered it would have learned how to dig through ancient ruins, brushing the dust from the tiny particles of shell and stone that make up the message's design; and later, that the find and the Form would be reported in magazines and produced in games; whereby it might catch the eye of a curious Symbolist, and perhaps win the heart of a responsive public.

Someday we may know how such fated events come to pass, with inexorable precision, fulfilling our needs and desires.

Until then... we just don't know.

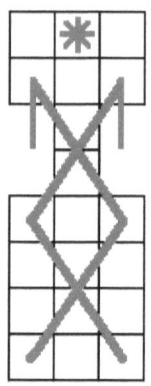

Dedicated
to the Cause of
Love and Peace

Part 2:

Prophecy and the Ur-Cult

by Walt Darring

The role of prophecy in society is two-fold: it predicts what will happen in the future, and it recognizes prophecies which have been fulfilled. The first role is a matter of predilection and faith, for even if one is convinced that a prophecy will be fulfilled, one is never sure what will actually happen, or when or how. The second role is a matter of fact, but also the cause of astonishment and undeniable wonder. In the Ur-Board Book, we indulge in both forms of prophecy, with due respect for the differences between them. The predictions of the future, we take with a grain of salt, and describe them in such a way that a reader might agree with it on the basis of today's world. But as for the confirmation of prophecies fulfilled— we speak of them in utmost seriousness, no matter how inexplicable they may seem. It is, after all, the role of a symbolist to distinguish between what is meaningful and what is willful; and the judge of his performance is the Reader. So, judge for yourself. And fear not; for if we are right, history is on our side.

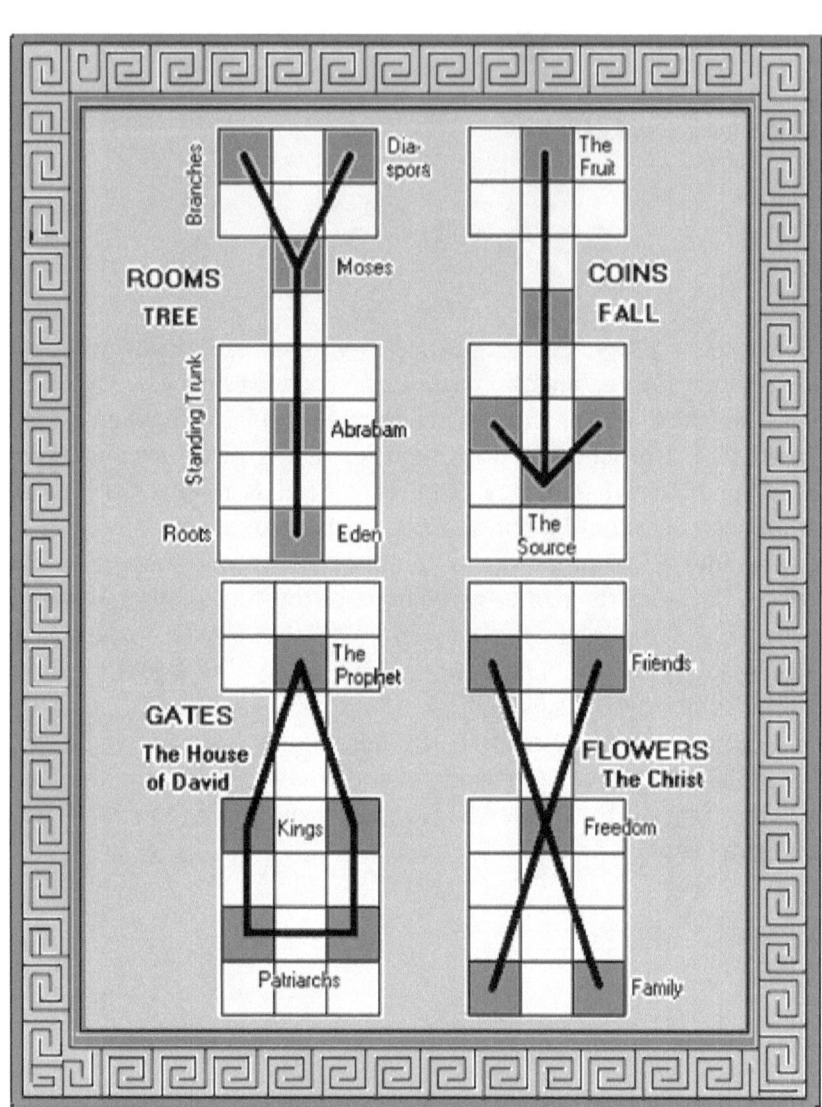

23. Biblical Revelation

We begin with what we know: What do we believe? Can the Ur-board tell us that?

There are four suits in the Ur-board.

What do they symbolize? What do they mean?

When we lay them out in canonical order— Rooms, Coins, Gates, and Flowers— each suit with its 20-square grid for context, immediately the four forms take shape before our eyes— a Tree-form, an Arrow pointing down, a House-form, and a large dominant X.

What do they mean?

Well, quite simply, these are the major themes of the Bible, captured in four symbols. The Old Testament is represented (in Rooms and Coins) by the Tree in the Garden of Eden, and a symbol of the Fall. And the New Testament is represented (in Gates and Flowers) by the House of David, and an X for the Christ.

Contemplate this in the quietness of your soul: the Tree, the Fall, the House, the X— are these not deeply etched archetypes of the Judaeo-Christian tradition? Yet they come to us from a source, more than two thousand years before Christ, indeed several centuries before Abraham— at the very verge of Pre-history.

These Biblical symbols have internal significance, too. For instance, the Rooms tiles distinguish between the original condition of Adam (Eden); the nomadic life of the tribes that took their family traditions from Abraham and Moses; and the widespread Civilization of the Human Race, that inherited or adopted their faith. The Coins symbolize the Fall; but it is ambivalent, for it may be associated with renewal, like falling fruit that nourishes the soil. The House takes its shape from the two Patriarchs (Abraham and Moses) and two Kings (David and Solomon) who uphold the pinnacle of the Messiah (Christ). And the X illustrates a concept of Freedom that begins when the person moves away from his Family (or tribe) to seek the company of his chosen Friends (the pagans).

Finally, the Suits comment on Economic issues, private and public: expanding Property and collapsing Wealth on the one hand, and beleaguered Security and confident Luxury on the other. We may find some meaning for the present world in this allegory.

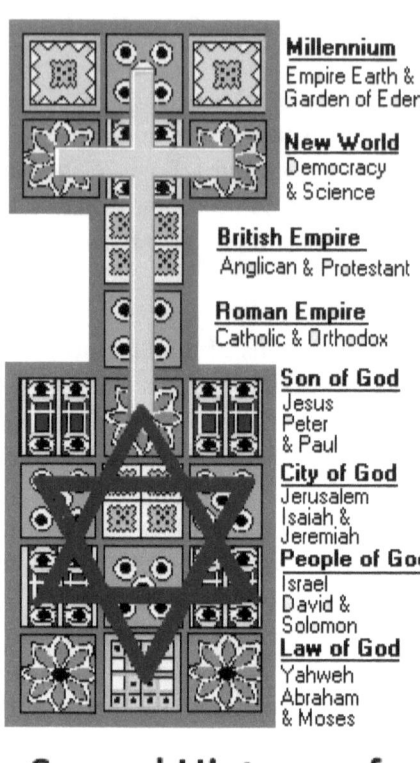

Millennium
Empire Earth &
Garden of Eden

New World
Democracy
& Science

British Empire
Anglican & Protestant

Roman Empire
Catholic & Orthodox

Son of God
Jesus
Peter
& Paul

City of God
Jerusalem
Isaiah &
Jeremiah

People of God
Israel
David &
Solomon

Law of God
Yahweh
Abraham
& Moses

Sacred History of
Western Civilization

Political History of
Western Civilization

Crown: Mystical **East**	Third Eye: **Secular Faith**	Crown: Magical **West**
Eye: **Popular Culture**	Face: **United States**	Eye: **Personal Conscience**
	Throat: **Revolutions**	Romantic Era
	Voice: **Protestant Faith**	Age of Reason
Shoulder: **Old World** Tradition	Heart: **Romantic Love**	Shoulder: **New World** Freedom
Arm: **Church: Arts**	Chest: **Feudal Valor**	Arm: **State: Sciences**
Hand: **Roman Church**	Belly: **Catholic Faith**	Hand: **Roman State**
Leg: **Christ** (Biblical)	Gate of Life **Cult of Madonna**	Leg: **Caesar** (Pagan)

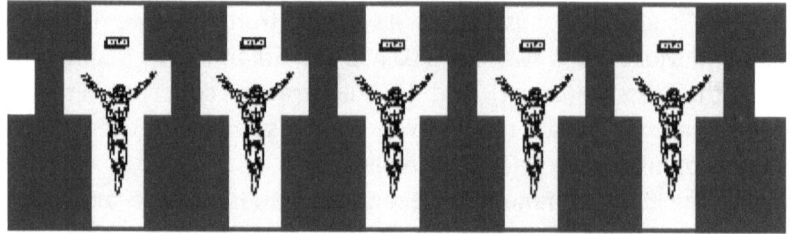

24. The Judaeo-Christian Tradition

But the Ur-board is capable of much more challenging general-izations. For instance, it depicts the Judaeo-Christian Tradition by accommodating its sacred symbols and adding allegorical values to them. The Star of David stands upon the bottom central tile (Gate of Life), a symbol of God's Law, its twelve spot design a symbol of the twelve tribes unified by the Torah, in the tradition of Abraham and Moses. Its inverted triangle extends upward to the establishment of Jerusalem, the City of God. The other triangle is based on the doctrine of the People of God, which reaches its apex in Jesus, the Son of God.

The Cross of Christianity stands upon the peak of that star, its trunk passing through the two empires of Christian history, the Roman and British empires; its arms reaching out to embrace the whole human race, as encouraged by Science and Democracy; and its head in the Millennium, where it inspires visions of a world at peace.

And the Ur-board also depicts Christian history by its analogy to the human body. The legs (or columns) of the Roman faith were Jesus Christ and Julius Caesar, the biblical and pagan roots of pantheistic Rome. Between them, they initiated a cult of the Madonna, the Mother of God, in celebration of unconditional love. From that cult arose the Catholic Faith, with its central ritual of the Eucharist, or Family Meal. During the Medieval age, Feudal competition accompanied the emergence of the arts and sciences. Finally, in the Renaissance, the courtly love tradition blossomed into the ideal of Romantic Love, the sentiment of a refined and educated nobleperson. But the Protestant sects of Christianity and the Democratic revolutions of the Romantic era, removed the ideal of True Love from the court of Privilege, and established it in the court of Law, where Popular Culture and Personal Conscience are working out a new Secular Faith, which will unify the population of Earth.

The Ur-board can symbolize this history because it was the spiritual progenitor of the Judaeo-Christian tradition, and (as we see in the bottom row of crucifixes) the Ur-board form is *the space between crosses*. The crosses symbolize the conscious aspect of history (the Triumphs of Man), and the Ur-board forms between them symbolize the subconscious River of Dreams, which flows beneath and between them.

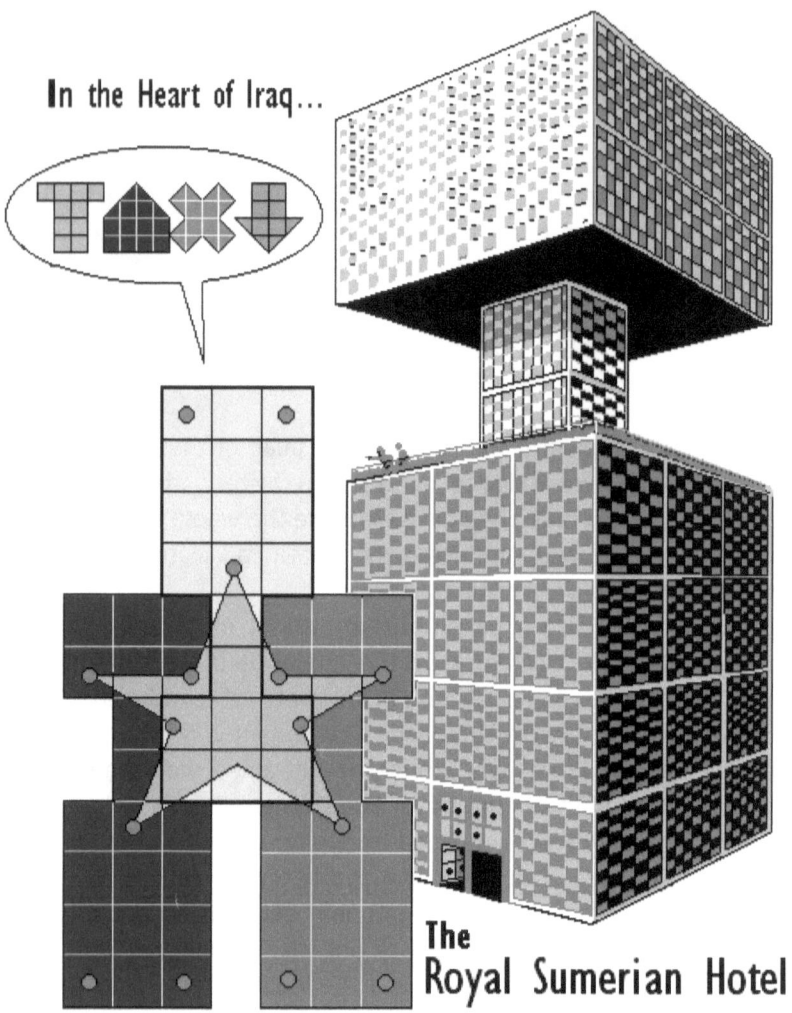

25. The Ur-cult

"Le cult, c'est moi"

Why would anyone make Ur-boards? Or play Ur-games? Or discuss the Ur-board? Well, ultimately, I suppose, there is one reason only, and that is, to *"honor the Form."* Which is to say, to apply the Form to countless uses, so that people will always remember the Ur-board.

That is my reason, and at the present moment, *I am the Ur-cult* (that is, I am the only one in it). But in the not-too-distant future, others will come along to swell the ranks of the Unaffiliated Ur-boarders of America. And when they are carrying out the mission of the cult, their motivation will be no different from mine. For how *can* it be? There's nothing to be gained by the use of the Form that couldn't be had without it; unless perhaps people find the Form attractive and buy into it. Then maybe you can make a profit by being a prophet. But though it may be used as a popular icon by anyone anywhere, the Form does not take sides on any issue, does not say do this or don't do that, but only what was said long ago, *"I am that I am."* And therefore, it will have the same message for everyone— *"Remember the Ur-board. Honor the Form."*

There need be no institution for the perpetuation of the cult's mysteries. Everything about the Ur-board appeals to a person's generous nature and genuine conviction.— Enjoy yourself, it says, study the board, contemplate its harmonies, its wit, its wisdom; and, of course, do what you can to *"honor the Form."*

It is my belief that by so doing, we are advancing the cause of Civilization in the world. For Civilization has been passed along to modern day Urthlings from one source in the past, but by many routes. Sometimes it spread through conquest, sometimes through trade, sometimes through religious conversion, or political alliance, or the spirit of the age. Now at a time when Civilization may be about to become a loose system of diverse local cultures, bound together for economic purposes but existing apart in villages where the people of each community govern themselves, it is only fitting that the task of spreading this Post-Historical Civilization should fall to an artifact designed by the gods or ancient wizards, the *ur-game board*— a board that children can play with, that adults might revere and use to symbolize their ideas, that the elderly may leave to us when they die, as a memento and perhaps a family heirloom.

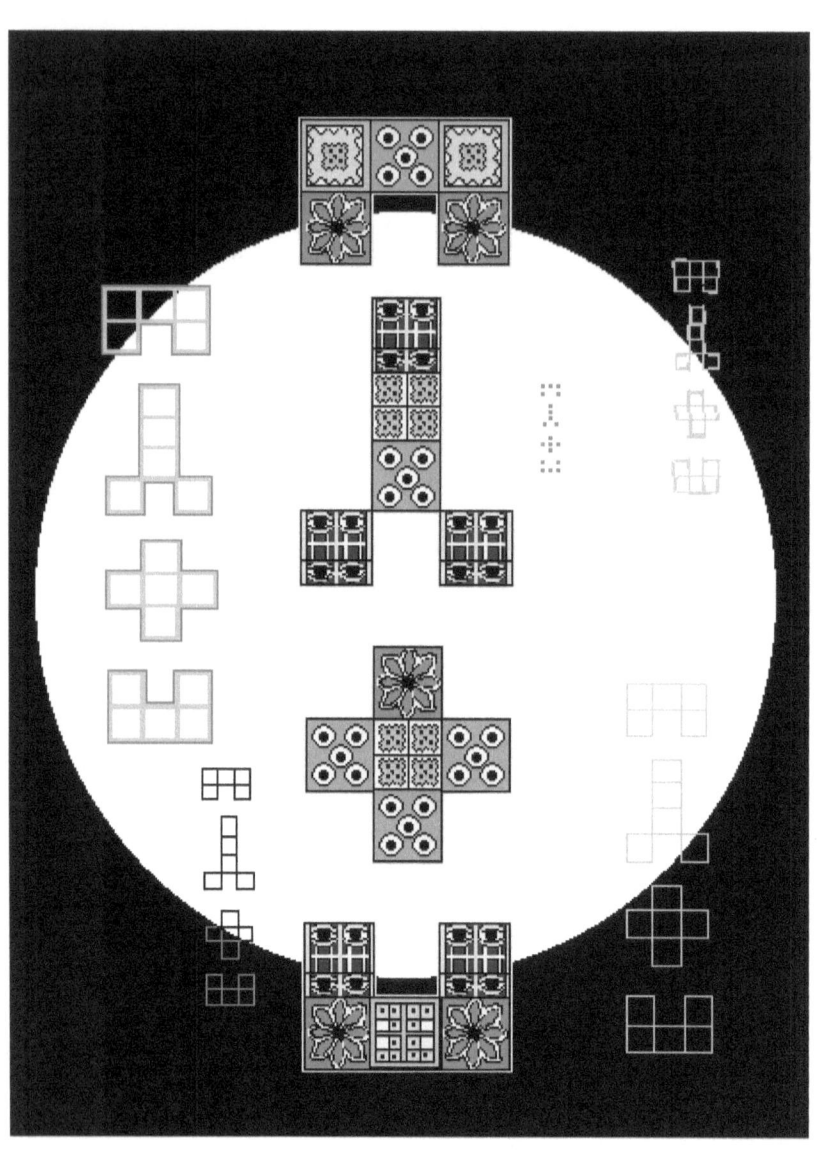

26. Urth and Its Colonies:
(What's to Become of Us?)

One day I thought to myself: "The Ur-board consists of twenty tiles. Four groups of five. What would we have if we let the groups take shape in whatever way seems best for symmetry and symbolism?"

Well, five tiles most readily form a bracket; so, with brackets at both ends of the board, we divide the middle tiles into two forms— a Cross and a Rocket!

I had stumbled upon the Ur-board's prophecy of the coming world.

What can we find in it? The bottom bracket is the Urth population (Gates), dwelling on a foundation of Democracy and Science (Flowers). Far from Urth, a Spaceship carries away most of Urth's population, to colonize the solar system and explore the local stars. Between the two populations is a "plus" sign. Though separated by billions of miles, the two people are united by a common culture.

The Urth is the Garden of Eden, the home to which families return after generations in Space; a human habitat where you can live outdoors, where ancient monuments, restored to their original splendor, adorn the Holy Land, and where you will hear talk of new science and new faiths for as long as the planet is tenable. In this Garden, female (erotic) values will prevail, in a global democracy of continental states.

But on the great ships, which travel through several generations to distant places and return to Urth in regular cycles, male (martial) discipline will unify the population. And the "colonies" they form will not belong to Urth, but will be autonomous worlds, trading with Urth for mutual benefits. And these isolated states must undergo the phases of history that lead to democracy.

*   *   *   *   *

Shortly after these reveries, I fell asleep and had a strange dream.

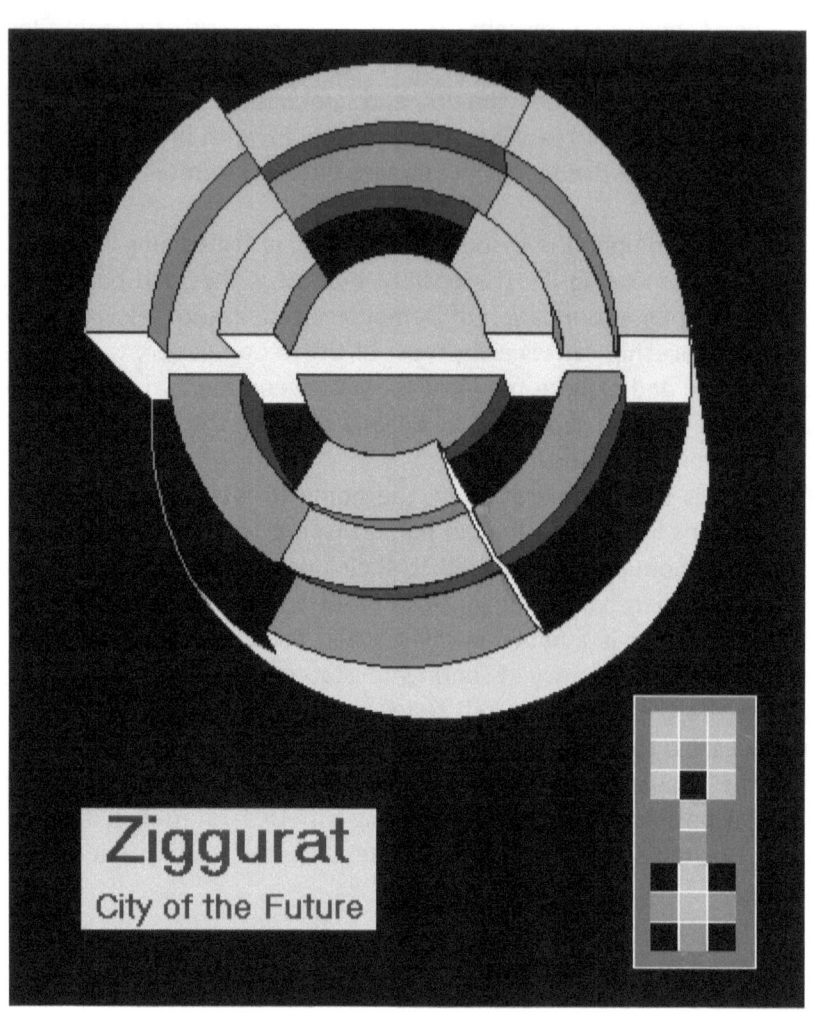

Ziggurat

City of the Future

27. The Ziggurat of Zanzibar

I was sitting at the window of a flying saucer. We were hovering over a structure which looked like a multi-tiered stadium. Actually, it was a mall—a huge mall, five miles wide and a mile high. The roof-system was composed of giant arc fragments, at four levels. The entire plant was powered by sunlight from solar receptors that covered the top (yellow) level, and by wind from the third (or red) level array of windmills. The second (green) level was covered with terraces of cultivated soil. And at the fourth (the blue) level were fresh water reservoirs. And that was only the roof!

After we landed on the wind-roof and were taken below, we gazed about at endless scenes of activity, in a panorama of immense perspective, illuminated from the roof and air-conditioned throughout. But it was as silent as a valley. Only local noises struck the ear, giving each area its own character in the immensity. Workers traveled in squads on the quiet streets, most of them young adults in uniforms. In some areas crowds flocked to places of culture and entertainment near the university campus, or to shops and restaurants surrounding the capitol, or to sports arenas, tourist attractions, and hotels.

It was a city of millions. Everything was contained and recycled within the mall. Just outside its towering walls, farm villages and wilderness covered the Urth with scenes of natural beauty, through which interstate highways wound between towns like prayer-beads.

But the remarkable thing about this city was that its design was a circular form of the Symmetrical Ur-board! A large field variously cultivated beside the city revealed the source of the design. I looked at the man sitting next to me and wondered aloud, "A Phase 7 board?"

"Oh yes," he said, smiling broadly. "They love the Form here."

But seeing that I was more perplexed than amused, he dropped his smile and asked with cool indifference what I thought about the Ur-cult.

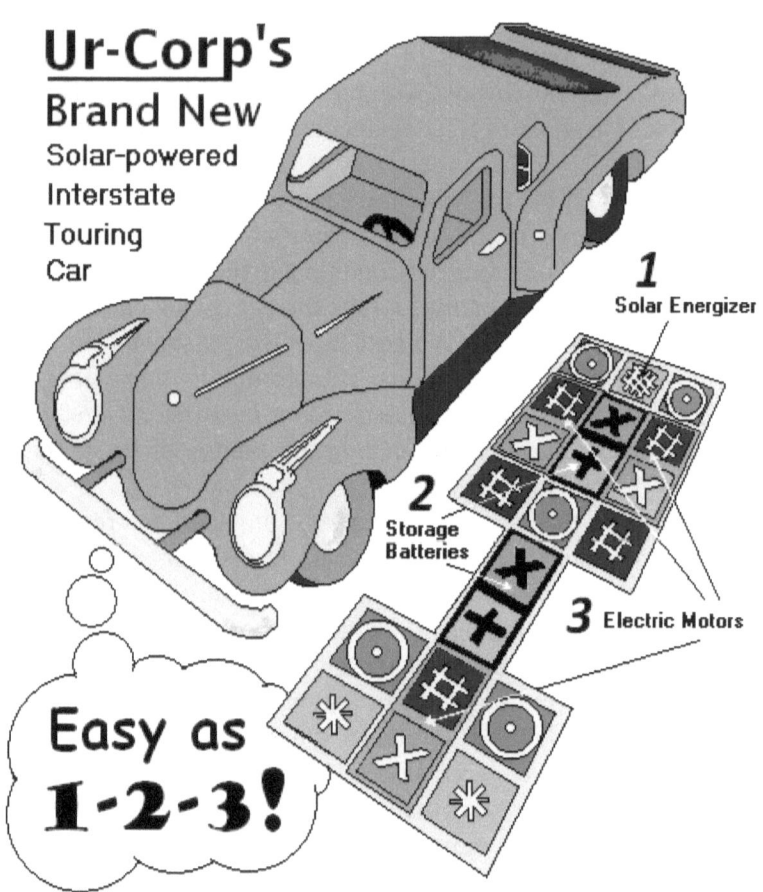

28. A Rental Car

"I know nothing about it," I said. "I'm from a different time."

"Ah, then you'll love it," he said, smiling again. "It's... well, it's silly, in a way... and yet, sublime. You are familiar with the Ur-board, I see. Yes, well, these people are dedicated to the game board, which they call the Form. They consider themselves disciples of a loose-knit spiritual cult, a sort of church. Oh, they are a very sensible people who lead productive lives, but they have one major idiosyncrasy, one distinguishing practice— they call it 'honoring the Form.' The trick is to solve a problem of design by using the Form. I mean a serious, practical problem. Of course, it has to work. In fact, you'll be suspected of fostering nonsense on the job if you do not demonstrate several advantages to the Ur-board design. But if it does work, it attracts the eye and charms the imagination of the public. People smile when they see it and accept it readily as a cultural icon."

Later, when I looked about in shops and furniture stores— I found Ur-board tables, Ur-board bedsteads, Ur-board mirrors and trellises. Not that there weren't many more different designs, but the Ur-corp products were conspicuous everywhere.

Like the car I drove to the village in. I rented it from a young girl, who was anxious to point out its features on the Ur-board chart. I laughed when I saw it, and she smiled and nodded. "Yes, an Ur-Car."

It was made of metallic plastic, and it handled beautifully. But I was surprised by the shape of the car— not at all compact and streamlined. Instead, it had an air of old-fashion innocence and candor, like early 20th Century technology. Ur-corp seemed to have cornered the market in humor and nostalgia.

There was no copyright or patent for the design. There was no money made on the use of its form. The Ur-cult was, as the man said, a loose association of "ur-boarders" who tried, in their jobs and homes, to honor the Form, to spread its image about, making Urth a free theme park without boundaries, and making the Ur-board itself a logo stamped on the work of others. Not on toys or souvenirs only, but on cities and cars.

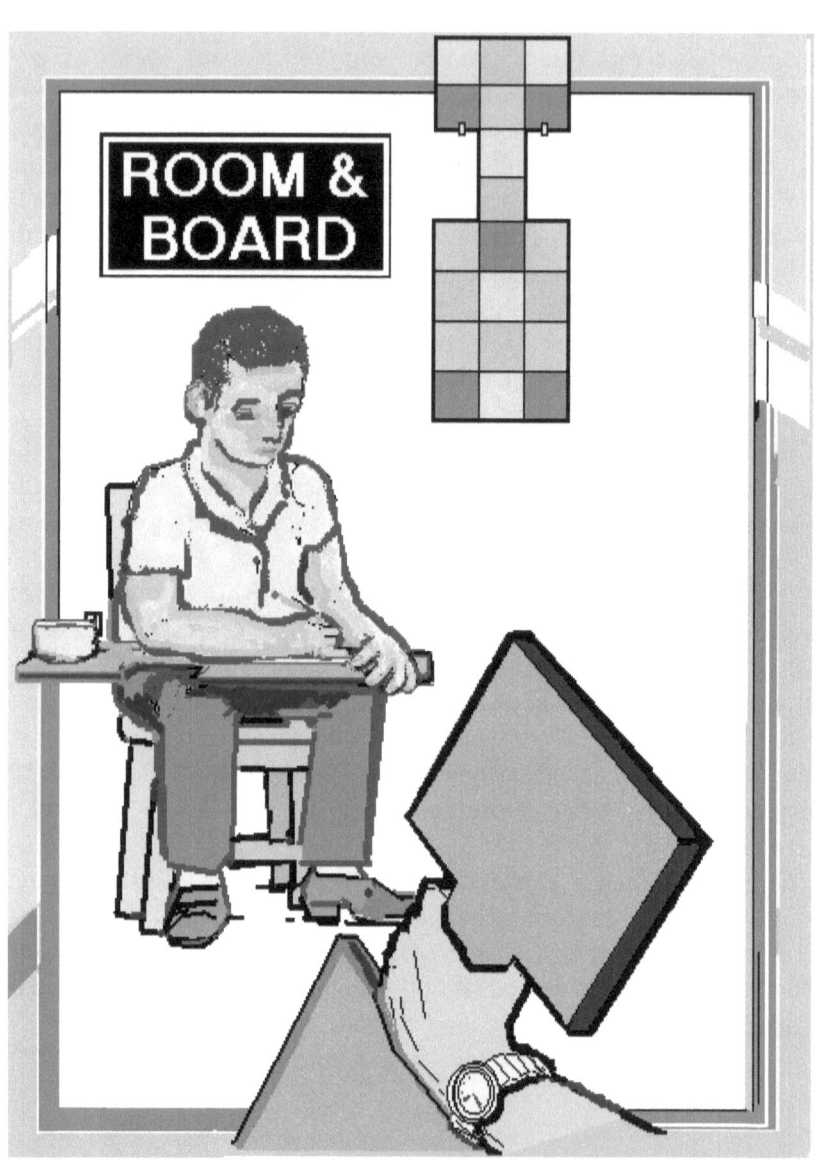

29. Hanging Around the House

The friend I was visiting in the village was an Ur-boarder. He and his wife and their two children played some high-spirited Ur-games one evening. But that was all. Most of the time their personal Ur-boards hung on the wall and were seldom noticed.

Their house was bare and quiet, carpeted throughout and sporting a few pieces of furniture. But there were no tables. Instead, when someone wanted to write or eat, he took a blank Form in his lap and went to work. The neck was used for handling the board— to adjust it while seated, or to carry it around. And the head often held drinks or instruments.

Once I watched my friend cook with an Ur-Chopping-board. He cut up the meat on the Ur-board's body, sliced vegetables on its head, and chopped seasoning on the neck. Then he carried it like a portable counter to the stove.

I asked my friend about the blank Forms. "Utility boards," he called them. And he showed me a closet where twenty of them, of uniform height and texture, were stacked, leaning against the wall. For small gatherings, he said.

He told me about one 'boarder who made a metal Ur-board to use at night in the city as a defensive shield. Wobbled rapidly before the face, it shielded the bearer from direct or overhead blows; and if the assailant tried to grab the board, he could twist it out of his grasp and hit him with it. "Did it work?" I asked. He chuckled: "I wouldn't try it."

He told me about Ur-furniture that was popular. A full-length bathroom mirror, for instance, with shelves on the shoulders for make-up and lotions. Also a fine wooden stand made of two blank Forms joined by canted shelves, with a magazine rack on the bottom and a book shelf on the top. He had just about run out of ideas when his children came in and said I should visit their school the next day.

"Yes, yes," he said. "Good idea."

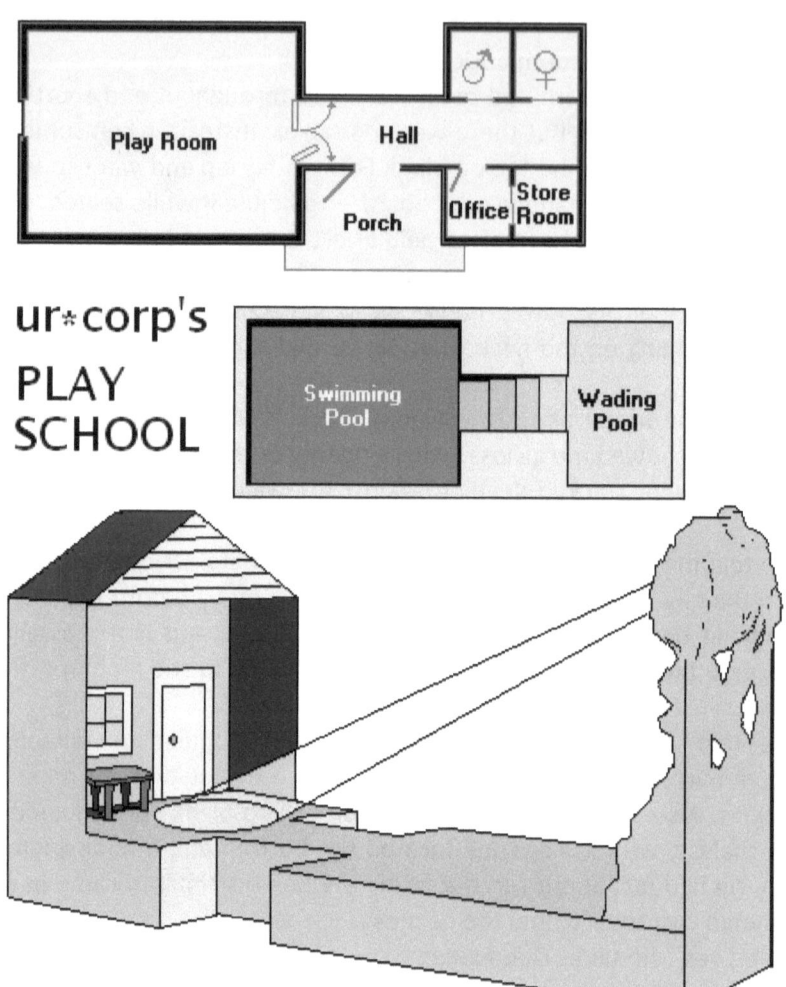

ur*corp's
PLAY
SCHOOL

30. The School Board

The school turned out to be a pre-school based on Montessori principles, which taught babies the basic skills of living and young children the creative arts. It was called a "Play School," because for the three years they attended the school, the children worked on a play to present their parents, to show the progress they had made. The children learned to read and write in order to compose the play. They learned carpentry and painting. They learned music, dance, and public speaking. And they wrote the play, built the props, and performed on a stage especially designed for that production.

It was here, in early school, that Ur-boarders hoped to instill in their children a love of the Form.

The school house had the floor plan of an Ur-board. You entered from a porch at the neck, where a hallway ran from the Play Room in the body to the office and restrooms in the head. The Play Room was where the children wrote, worked on, practiced, and produced the play, which would be presented at the end of the school year along with other evidence of the children's progress.

The stage, shaped like an Ur-board, featured a home scene in the head and an open field scene in the body, with a bridge between them. Children moved about on stage at the height of the adult directors, who could stand near them in the bay without getting on stage.

After school each day, students would cool off in a pool shaped like an Ur-board, with wading in the head, swimming in the body, and steps in the neck between them.

My friend's younger child went to that school. His older child went to a school that prepared him to leave home in a year or two and enter a boarding school. From there he would travel the world with other youths and eventually enter the work force of a city.

Ur-Charts
No. 43
Art and Communication

Letter Chart

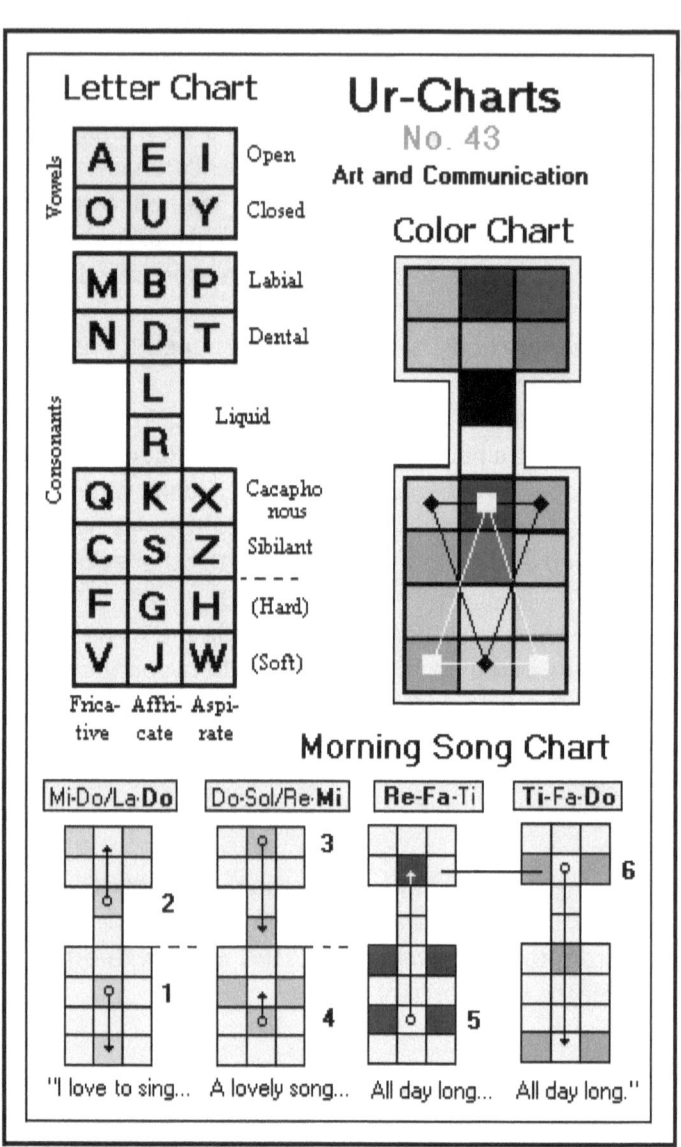

Vowels

| A | E | I | Open |
| O | U | Y | Closed |

Consonants

| M | B | P | Labial |
| N | D | T | Dental |

| L | | Liquid |
| R | | |

Q	K	X	Cacaphonous
C	S	Z	Sibilant
F	G	H	(Hard)
V	J	W	(Soft)

Frica-tive   Affri-cate   Aspi-rate

Color Chart

Morning Song Chart

Mi·Do/La·Do   Do·Sol/Re·Mi   Re·Fa·Ti   Ti·Fa·Do

2   1   3   4   5   6

"I love to sing...   A lovely song...   All day long...   All day long."

31. The Lesson Plan

I asked if the older child's school had as many Ur-things in it.

"More," she said. "We have *The Ur-board Book*, which we study with a fellow student. But that's a recess activity. And we have the Ur-board Club, that sponsors Ur-naments, and has Ur-board exhibits and awards. This year's winning Ur-board was made of marble and sculpted with a laser chisel. And— let's see, we have the Ur-Scotch competition..."

"The school indoctrinates you in the beliefs of the Ur-Cult?"

"Yes. It's an Ur-School. But mostly we study mathematics, mechanics, electronics, and other sciences to prepare for college. And we have map-drawing classes, to prepare for world travel, and cultural history. And we have Art and Communication classes— that's mostly where the Ur-board comes in. Wait, I have an Ur-Chart here."

She groped about in her voluminous purse and pulled out a cardboard lesson card.

"You see," she said, pointing to features on the card, "there are the six vowels and twenty consonants in a meaningful arrangement on the Ur-board. Next to that are the four suits, forming basic music patterns into a song. (Here she sang it, hastily.) We sing it every morning. Boys do one suit, girls the next. And next to that is the Color-Chart..."

"What's this?" I asked about a chart on her desk.

"That's the Taxi System— a universal sign language. The Blue House marks waiting areas and holding patterns, where people are sitting, parking, or not yet in motion. The Yellow T marks the traffic areas, where workers or vehicles pass, or times when people are en route to their destination. The Green Arrow, used with a name or another symbol, points the way to it. The Red X means you have arrived."

"My God," I said to my friend, "this is too much! You people are being brain-washed by a Symbol! You have to die to get away from Ur-boards!"

We laughed genially. Then when he saw I might be halfway serious about it, he shrugged: "It's just a game board."

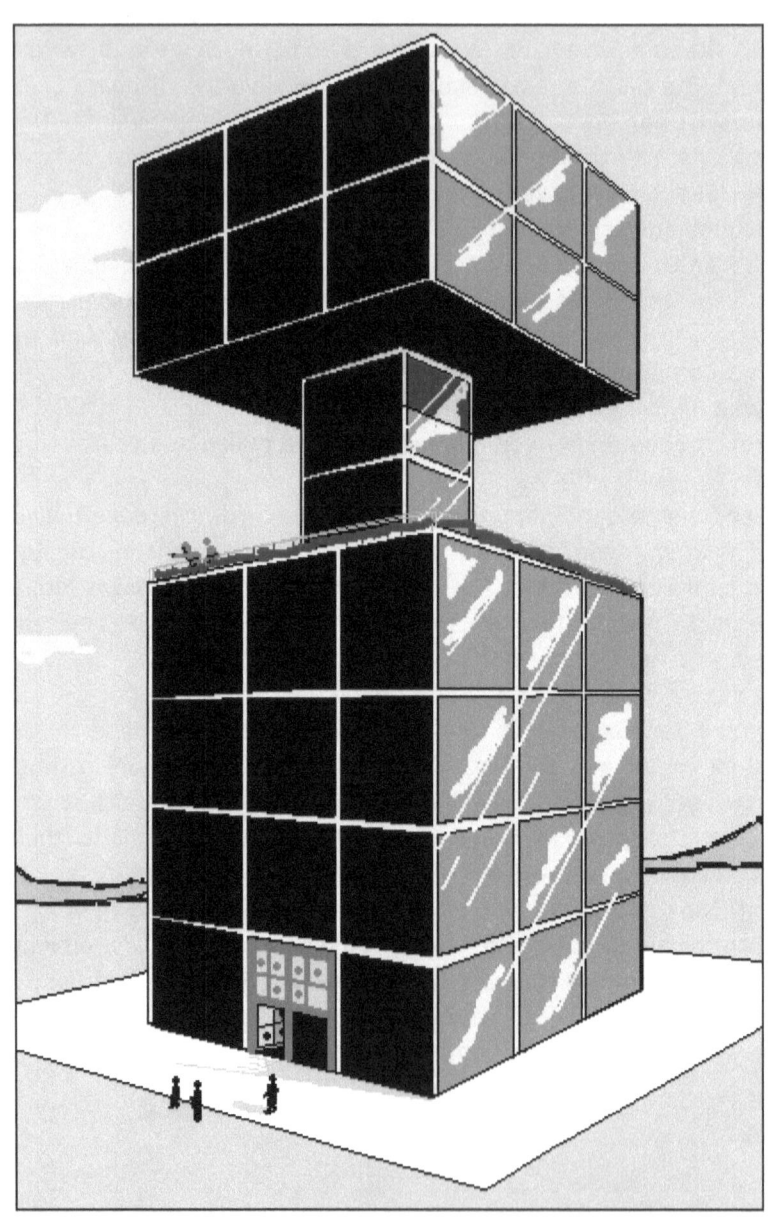

32. The Ur-Church

But I don't think so, not after I visited the Ur-Church.

The building was eight stories tall, and it towered over the grassy hilltop like a giant overlooking its domain. Covered in large squares of Antique Black marble, it mirrored the clouds and cast an ebony Form against the sky.

It did not always look like an Ur-board. On two holidays during the year, the head was lowered by hydraulic pumps in the neck, until it rested upon the shoulders of the building. Then the upper museum, which contained the priceless art treasures of the community, was open to the public. At the end of the day, the head was returned to its position, to await the next holiday.

What were the priceless art treasures of the upper museum? To appreciate that, you would have to know about the contents of the lower museum.

As we approached the building, I remember saying to my friend, "So this is where people are buried."

"Oh no," he said, "people prefer cremation. Some states require it, to save space for the living. No, this is where the Ur-boards of the dead are kept."

"Kept where? In storage?"

"No, on the walls. They are exhibited as works of art. And people come from all over the world to commune with the dead, in countless Ur-Churches throughout the land. Every Ur-board is tagged with its owner's name and dates, and is kept on the walls for fifty years. Then, if the board is chosen as a work of art, or if it belonged to a famous person, it is moved upstairs into the upper museum. Otherwise it is... stored, I guess, or sold. Here's the bronze Gate of Life. Let's go in."

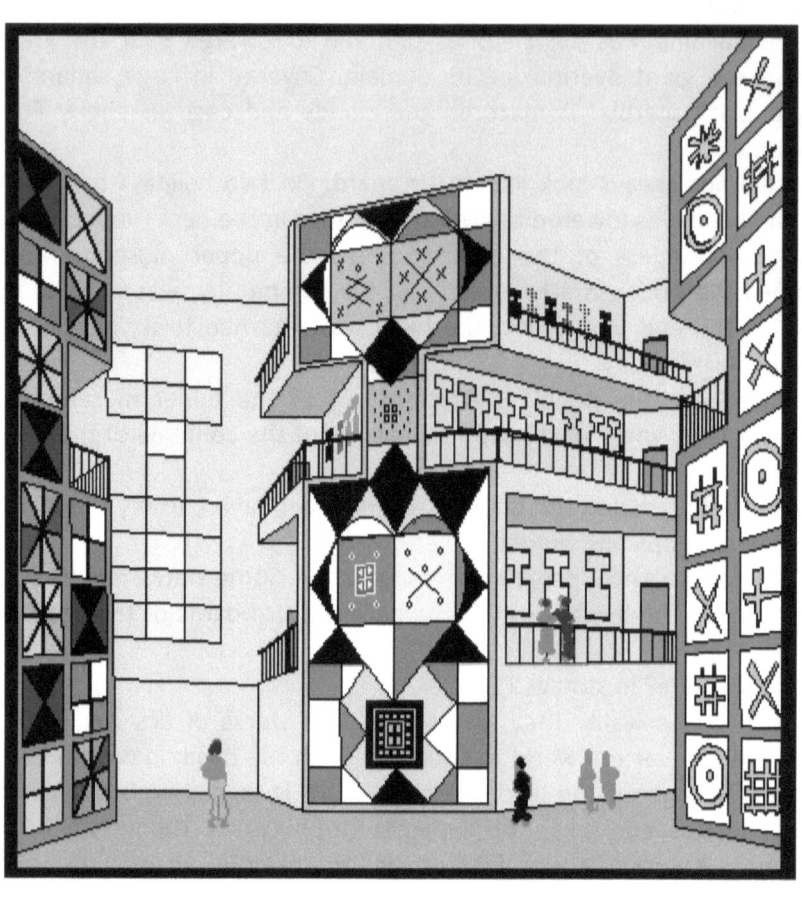

Interior of an Ur-Church

33. Interior of an Ur-Church

We entered and found ourselves in a vast empty room, four stories tall, with hardwood floors and an atmosphere of perfumed silence. We were completely walled in by four monumental Ur-boards, of various and unusual designs, executed by local artists. On the walls that swept back from these figures hung hundreds of Ur-boards, of all types and materials— wood, metal, ceramic, stone.

Everyone, it seems, had a "personal Ur-board." Often it was one the person had made and played with all his life— a prized possession, cherished like a friend. Sometimes it was commercially made, or the commissioned work of a well-known artist; more often it was the product of the person's careful craftsmanship. So, when the person passed away, his or her Ur-board entered the mausoleum and took its place beside the folk art of the century. There, on a wall in one of the galleries, it would be admired by generations of Urthlings, traveling about the world to commune with the Spirit of the Age.

It was not uncommon to see pilgrims— some in the long day of youth, some in the evening of old age— standing about for hours in contemplation of handmade Ur-boards. I spoke with some of them. Many did not think of the hanging Ur-boards as works of art, but met them as one would encounter strangers on a journey, enjoying their company.

* * * * *

I woke from the solemn reverie induced by the Ur-Church and found myself out of the dream at last. The future faded from memory, and I was left to face the past again.

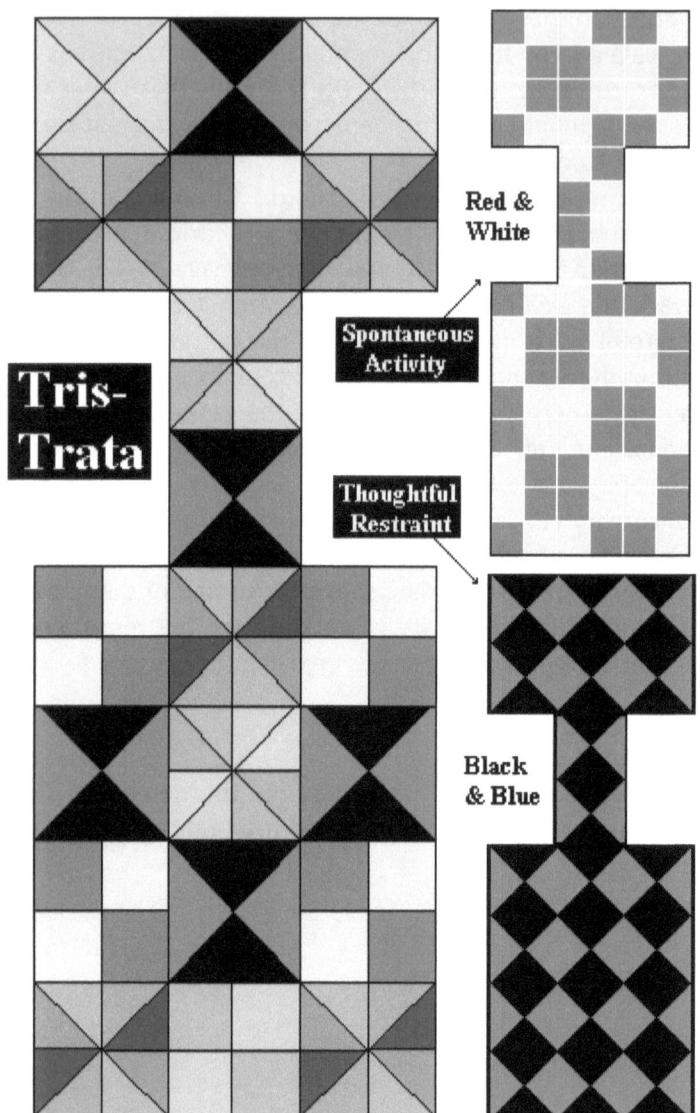

Tris-Trata

Red &
White

Spontaneous
Activity

Thoughtful
Restraint

Black
& Blue

34. Tris-trata: The Emotional Life

There were four great Ur-boards standing at the head of the galleries in the Ur-Church. The first one, which was behind us in the picture, was the Sumerian Ur-board. The other three were designs of dubious origin, which were adopted in the future as special Ur-board forms, meant to enhance contemplation by revealing the inner workings of this ancient prophetic artifact.

The first was Tris-trata, an analysis of the emotional life. The name veils its meaning somewhat, for it means "Tri"-strata, but is pronounced "Tris"-trata. The strata are the three levels of experience. The middle layer, first. It is the red and white matrix of youthful feeling, a symbolic representation of optimism, enjoyment, innocence, enthusiasm, confidence, laughter, and play. The deeper layer is its opposite: the black and blue texture of mature thought, a symbolic representation of concern, reflection, wisdom, sadness, suffering, and doubt. Finally, there is the superficial level, the ideas, beliefs, images, clichés, memories, judgments—one's conscious life.

Whenever your thoughts concern Life in any form (a life experience, a vital concern, a feeling of love or sorrow), you might sit before this oracle and let your eyes wander over its colorful form, absorbing its meanings, until you feel peaceful and whole.

During our visit to the Ur-Church, groups of people roamed the galleries, passing slowly by the Ur-boards that hung on the walls; they streamed along the stairs and aisles; some stopped to hear lectures about treasured boards in the collection; and there were always crowds, large or small, gathered in the foyer, standing around in the silent space across from Tris-trata, communing in her presence.

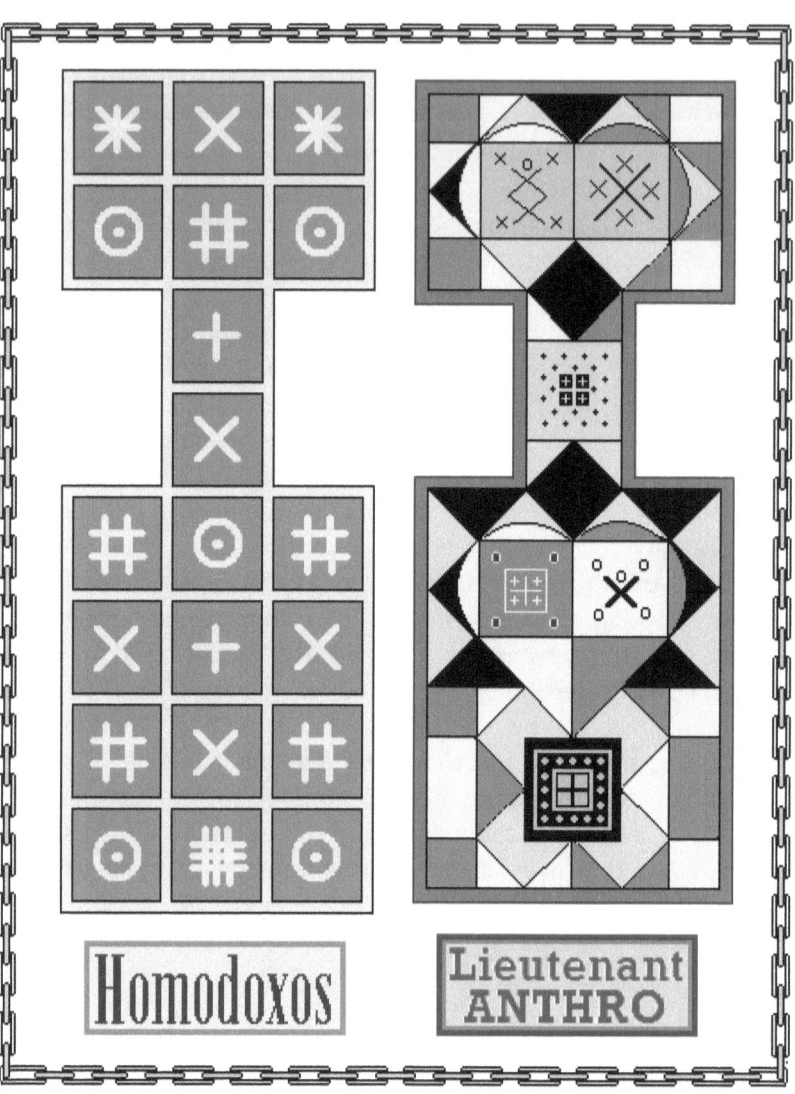

Homodoxos

Lieutenant ANTHRO

35. The Owl and the Lieutenant

The other two Ur-boards are for contemplation of a different kind. They are meant for the resolution of problems.

Homodoxos (the so-called "human truth") offers you advice for reasoning about relationships— family, neighborly, at school or at work, in love or in business. The simplicity of the design is its defining feature. It stands there like a wiseacre owl, saying "Who? Who?" But it isn't an owl. It's a child.

Homodoxos is not, as you might have expected, a wise old man. He is a comic character, called "the Kid." His hair sticks out like straw. His features are plain and simple. He is wide-eyed with wonder. And he's a bit shy about the patch of hair gro'in' on his groin.

His tile symbols represent the child's game of jacks. In the Flowers suit, you get an overhead God's-eye view of your activity; in the Quarters subsuit, you get the same activity as others see it, or as you envision it in yourself; in the Stars subsuit, you see the wobbling jack, struggling to spin, and coming to a stop; in the Gate of Life, you see the jack in its box, standing as if alive, upheld by memory and desire. The Coins suit shows the jack in stasis, asleep or dead. And the Gates suit shows the box, the bed or coffin.

Homodoxos is the candid child, the honest critic. He tells you what you know and helps you face it.

Lieutenant Anthro is an admired officer, before whom you tend to cease your petty complaints, your pretentious behavior, your feelings of envy and contempt for others, because he has none of these flaws. His personality is noble, courageous, and wise. The emblems on his uniform are designs taken from the elements of the six tile designs: the Gate of Life his buckle; Gates and Coins his medals of honor; Quarters symbolic of the Empire; and Stars and Flowers in his eyes.

The Good Lieutenant rarely has to speak. He lets you talk, and when you are done, he looks at you. That's all. You work it out.

The people in the Ur-Church assured me from their own personal experience that these meditation techniques have worked wonders, for them and their friends. I don't know, I've never tried them. I only tell you what I saw and heard.

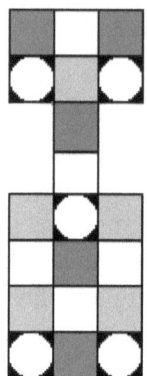

Dedicated
to Ur-chins
everywhere

Part 3:

Playing
Ur-Games

by Walt Darring

There's probably no better way to bond with a person of like persuasion than to play a table game, just the two of you— cards, dice, checkers, chess, backgammon. It becomes a custom, a ritual, a casual celebration of your friendship. Even more so when the game board is the product of your art, handmade, with familiar and unique designs. And more yet, when the board is the symbol of an idealistic cause, which advances youthful virtues in the world.

And yet— it is only a game. Nothing prevents an unfamiliar person from joining in and, enjoying the advantages of beginner's luck, begins beating you at your own game! The Sumerian Ur-board is specifically designed for that sort of play: all the games are easy to learn, they're fast and soon over, and Fate determines the outcome.

So Ur-board games don't measure your skill at play; they measure other winning qualities that you sometimes have and sometimes don't— confidence, enthusiasm, interest. The Ur-board taps into those sources of energy, and grants the win as Fate would have it.

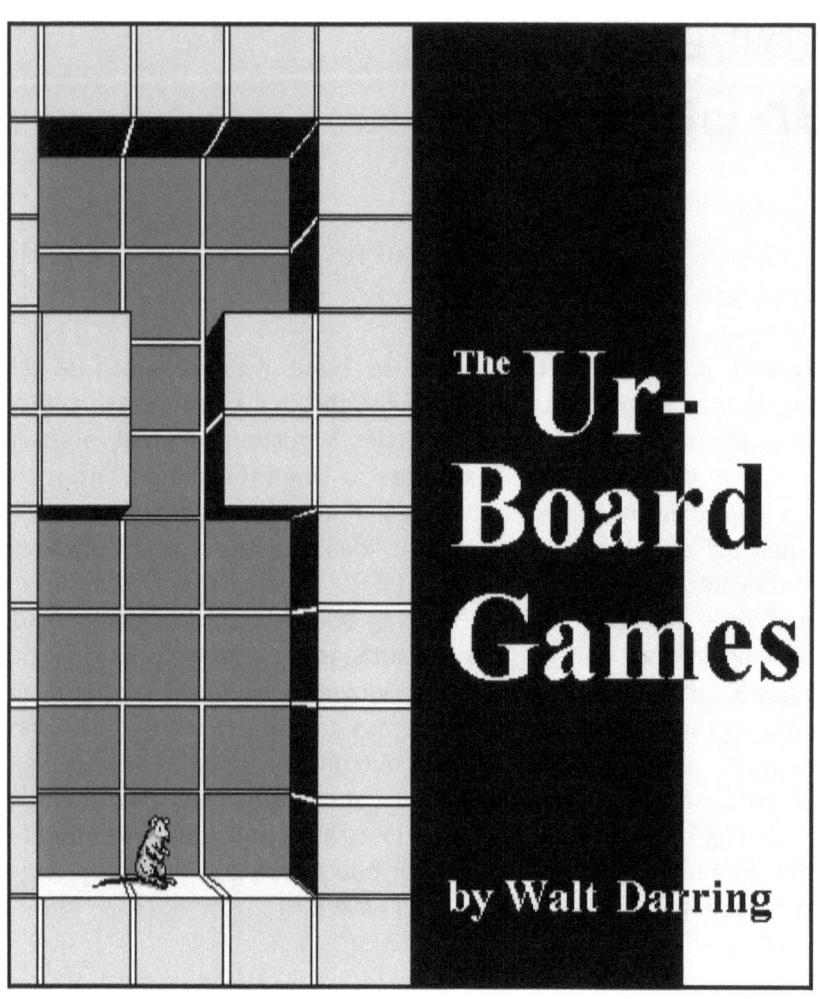

The Ur-
Board
Games

by Walt Darring

36. The Ur-Board Games

The following section of the Ur-board Book is intended to serve as a Rulebook to refer to as you learn to play. Even before you play, however, you can get an idea of the variety of games and their inner logic by looking through the descriptions and rules of the games.

These games are the result of forty years of symbolic interpretation and play with the Ur-board. They represent attempts, not to invent games for the board, but to find the games implied by the Ur-board's design.

Each game is a concept for play. As you work with the concept, the board itself tells you what must be done. So, all you have to do is set up the markers and begin playing according to the purpose and design of each game. Once you are familiar with the concept, you will be able to recall the rules by reviewing in your mind the logic of the game.

The typical Ur-game is brief and intense. A group of nine different Ur-games played in an evening can be an hour's diversion. But while you play, you cannot do other things (watch TV, have a conversation, read) or the games will become pointless and boring. You have to take time out and concentrate on each roll, *yours and your opponent's*. Then, when you do, you notice more than the competition; you notice the beauty of the thing— the coincidences, the symmetries, the perfect rolls.

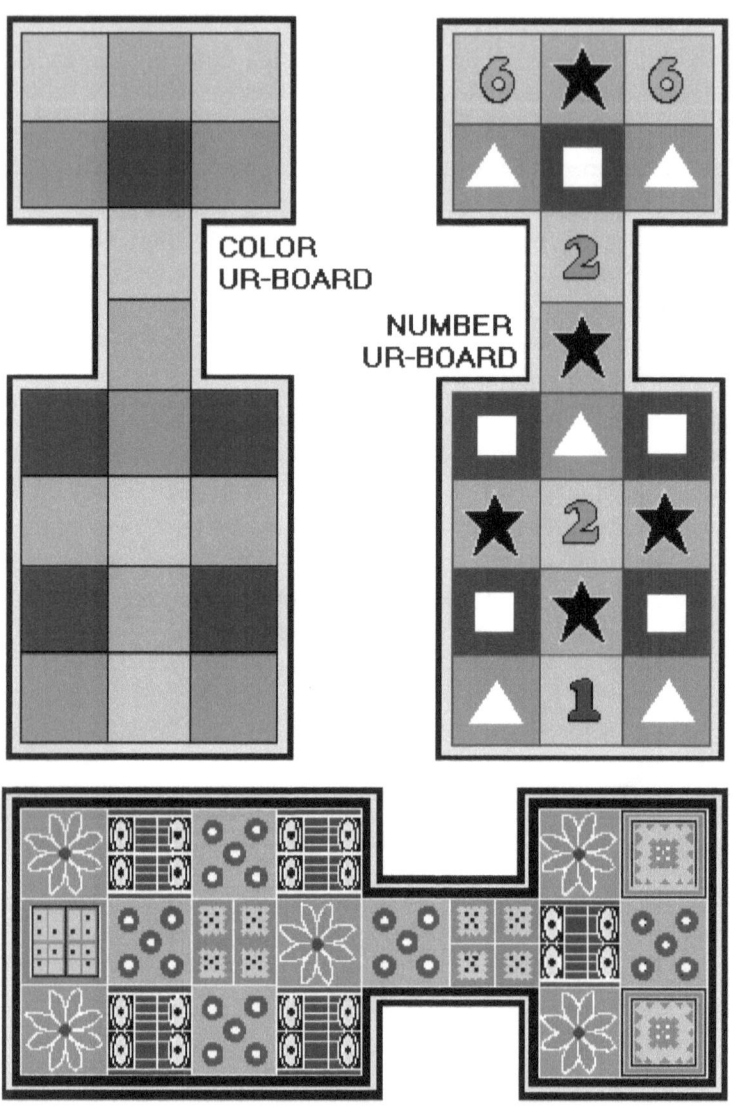

COLOR
UR-BOARD

NUMBER
UR-BOARD

TRADITIONAL UR-BOARD

37. Three Kinds of Ur-board

Before you can play an Ur-game, you must have an Ur-board.

Well, that's not entirely true. I have played Ur-Chase with experienced players, using no board or markers. Having memorized the tiles on the Chase-path (which is real easy, you learn it simply by playing the game often enough), we could just roll two dice and tell our opponent how to move the markers. Before the opponent rolls, he sums up the board (who is on the board, and where) and the score (how many are off, for both sides)... and so they continue. It's good for a long car drive.

But still, you need an Ur-board, to play the games as you learn them. You have three options. You can, of course, make a traditional Ur-board. And I encourage you to do that, some time before you die. But it's a difficult chore, to draw and trace the twenty symbols, and paint them, and give the whole a finished look.

But there's no reason why you need to have more than the Color Ur-board. You don't even have to use the official color scheme. Any set of four, five, or six colors will do, as long as they mark off the suits and subsuits meaningfully.

Actually, when you're familiar with the board, you don't need *any* colors. You can play all of the games on an empty Ur-board grid. You can draw an empty grid with pencil and ruler, in one inch tiles; it fits a sheet of paper perfectly; and you can have dimes and pennies for markers. You do need dice.

But still, you should have an Ur-board with distinctive tile designs, because you never know when you will want to teach a beginner, who needs the full complement of symbols. However, instead of using the Sumerian tiles, you can replace them with the Number Board. To avoid having a jumble of numbers on the board, it replaces 3, 4, and 5 with their geometric forms (the triangle, the quadrangle, and the pentangle) and uses numbers only for the Rooms suit. That way you are be able to run your eyes over the board and tell immediately what's on the board and where.

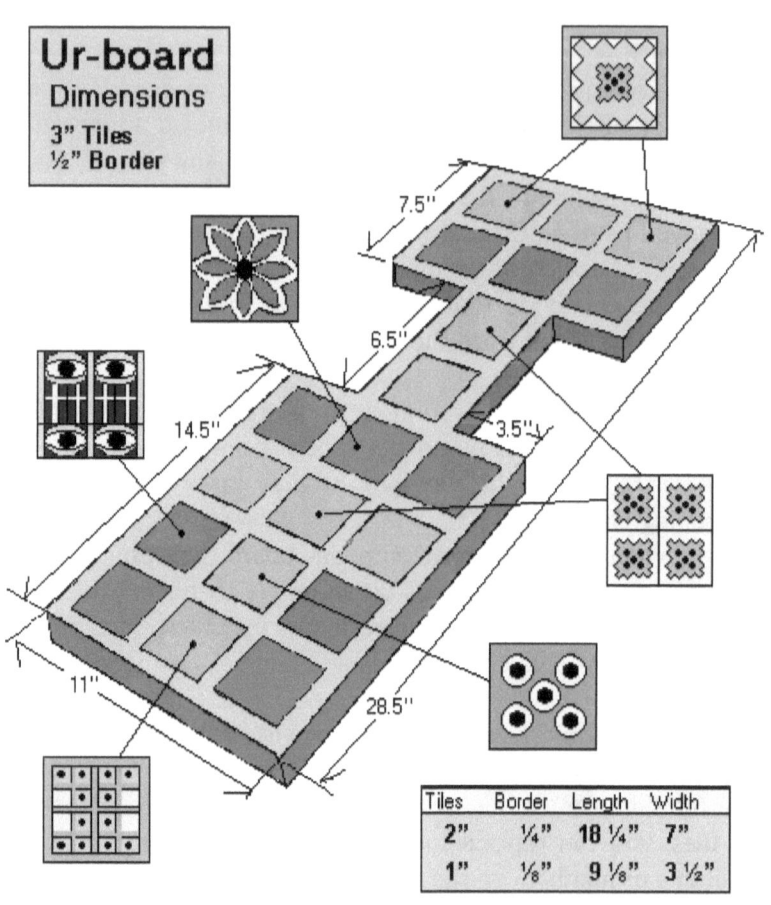

Ur-board
Dimensions
3" Tiles
½" Border

7.5"

6.5"

3.5"

14.5"

11"

28.5"

Tiles	Border	Length	Width
2"	¼"	18 ¼"	7"
1"	⅛"	9 ⅛"	3 ½"

38. Three Sizes of Ur-boards

There are also three standard sizes of Ur-boards, indicated by the size of the tiles. The sizes are 3 inches, 2 inches, and 1 inch.

The 3-inch board is good for displaying on the wall, or for playing games before audiences, large or small. It has a half-inch border all around, which clearly distinguishes the tiles at a distance. It is 28½ inches tall and 11 inches wide. But the neck is only 4 inches wide, so you can grasp it around the neck to carry it about.

The 2-inch board has a ¼ inch border. It is good for quiet, intimate play. Doubloons or casino chips fit nicely on the board as markers, whereas the stately 3-inch board requires something larger. The thin marker in close spaces on the 2-inch board may prove awkward for guys with large hands, but it's still manageable.

The 1-inch board has a ⅛ inch border. It is for traveling. Pennies and dimes work perfectly for markers.

*Something should be said about the materials appropriate for use in making an Ur-board. We have been talking wood, because we're thinking of playing games on it; wood is light and durable, easy to cut and paint, and soft to the touch. But since the Ur-board is also a work of art or craft, there are also plaster, plastic, ceramics, glass, aluminum, tin, marble, brick, cement, Styrofoam, ice, cardboard, and so forth.

An Ur-board birthday cake would be nice, for the right person. A fan. A kid, most likely, but not necessarily.

An Ur-board tombstone would be— well, weird at first, but elegant. It would look good among conventional tombstones. After four and a half thousand years of being dead, she should be good at it.

Future researchers, discovering your Ur-board in some ancient landfill, will say— "This one is old, very old. It stems from the early days of the 21st Century, about a year after the Resurrection. This is a memorial of one of the pioneer devotees of the cult that has virtually inherited the Earth. It must have cost no more than a few dollars to make back then. Today, it's worth millions."

Your Ur-board! Worth millions!

But you'll never see a penny of it. Oh, the ironies.

Ur-Chase

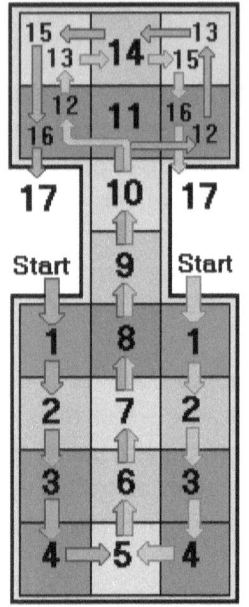

Make a mad dash to Finish! Get all seven markers off before your opponent does. Roll your dice and move your markers along the Chase Path. Continue rolling for your turn until you have to stop (see rules). If your marker lands on a tile your opponent occupies, remove his marker to start. And there are tiles that if you land on them, you can remove his markers (see rules). You have to roll the exact number to go off. First person to get his last marker off wins, but opponent has one complete turn to get his final markers off and tie the game.

The Chase Path

In Ur-Chase, no matter how far you are behind, you can always catch up and win the game! One-die throws for children just learning to count; two-dice throws for a fast adult game; three and four dice throws to challenge your speed at play.

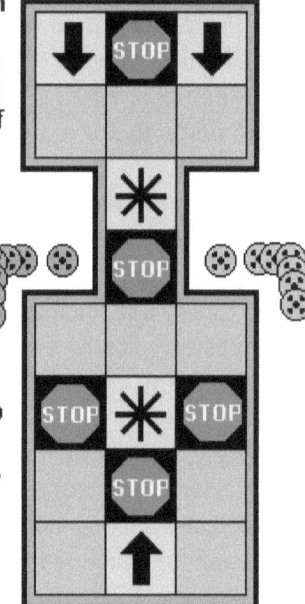

The Chase Board

39. Ur-Chase

Choose to play one-die or two-dice Ur-Chase.

Roll to see who goes first, and begin playing.

Remember, in Ur-Chase you keep rolling, you don't alternate.

You roll until you have to stop. Two things make you stop:

1. If you land on a Coins, or
2. if you have to bring on another marker

when you already have one on the board.

You have to roll the exact number to go off. If your number is too high, you have to bring on a new marker instead, and so end your turn. But you shouldn't bring on a new marker for any other reason; your best hope is to keep running. When you go off, you can bring on a new marker and continue rolling, because then you don't have a marker already on.

The Rooms tiles are used to knock your opponent's markers off and return them to Start. The Gate of Life, if you land on it, knocks off all your opponent's markers in the center shaft. The two Stars tiles in the head let you knock off all your opponent's markers in their respective side. And the Quarters tiles are "snipers." They knock off one of your opponent's markers any where on the board. If you land on a Quarters tile when your opponent has a sniper on it, you knock off the sniper and another marker, if there is one on the board.

*Ur-Chase is Number One, the Lead-off Player in the Ur-nament of Life. But it wasn't the first game we discovered. Ur-Check was the first game we played. The occasion was a family picnic. I was showing someone the four suits, or the chase path, when a cousin asked, "How do you play the game? Show me." I said I'd try, and we started rolling and explaining each rule as we made it up; by the time the game was over, we had what we would later call, "Ur-Check." At the time, we called it, "Ur." When couples came to visit, we'd end up playing Ur; and since the adults were using the Family Ur-board, the kids made their own. Then they set about to play a game, and in a few days, they had invented a game we would later call "Ur-Chase." The kids called it, "Ur." When they showed us their Ur-game, we began playing it ourselves. And since then Ur-Chase has become one of our favorite games.

Ur-Check

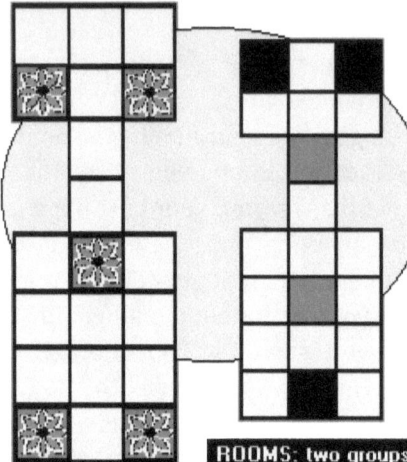

This is the classic Ur-game, like Ur-Chase, but more mature and deliberate. You alternate throws, and consider possible moves, playing offense and defense with each turn. All tiles participate in the basic strategies shown below, of Jumping, Checking, & Pushing Up. The game is played with two-dice throws, and moves are designed to keep your opponent away from the Finish line and you advancing toward it. The Flowers tiles act as safe areas where you can wait for the right number to get you off the board.

There is a one-die version of Ur-Check, but it is too scrappy, all the conflict focused on the opening moves, with very little opportunity for strategic play. Three and four dice Check are the opposite, tending to end up in gridlock. But Ur-Check fits the form perfectly— so well that at times it seems more like ritual than conflict.

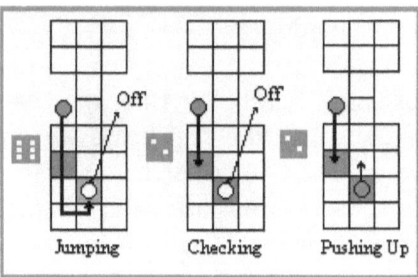

Jumping   Checking   Pushing Up

40. Ur-Check

Roll to see who goes first.

Each player gets one roll at a time. You can move two markers, one for each die rolled, or one marker the total of both dice. The object of play is to move steadily up the Chase Path, but pausing at times to keep your opponent off the center shaft, from which he can always go off. There are three rules of play:

Jumping. If you land on a tile occupied by your opponent, remove his marker and return it to Start.

Checking. If you land on a suit occupied by one of your opponent's markers, remove and return it to Start.

Pushing Up. You cannot land on a tile which you already occupy. But if you land on a suit which you occupy, push that marker up. As a result, you may jump or check or push up, and as a result, jump, check, or push up, in a chain reaction.

Two things to note about the suits in Ur-Check:

1. **Flowers** are safe, and
2. **Rooms** are divided into two sub-suits, as shown in the illustration. So, the Gate of Life jumps, checks, or pushes up only with the two Stars; and the Quarters do the same with each other.

*There is a chatter that occurs during an Ur-Check game, in which people (players and watchers) express their recognition of what has just happened, with descriptive remarks. This habit has resulted in a "glossary of terms," which would have proved useful if I had compiled it. But that's okay. The terms still exist, they're just not accessible to the public. Well, not yet.

A noteworthy instance of such jargon appeared this month in the now defunct *Annals of Analysis*. Chiefly, the article concerns a trivial but important matter: "If you roll a 3 and a 1, don't just jump to four; instead, jump to 3 first, then to 1, which *gives* you the four— plus Gates. And that lowly Gates, if it survives, may affect the outcome of the game.

So, "Grab your Gates," my friend! It is not just your natural impulse, not just a great slogan for a political party, not just good advice for this part of town—"Grab your Gates" sums it all up! If you see something out of place, or left unfinished, or overlooked— don't just sit there trembling, stand up and shout— "Grab your Gates!"

Ur-Chock

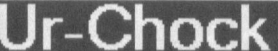

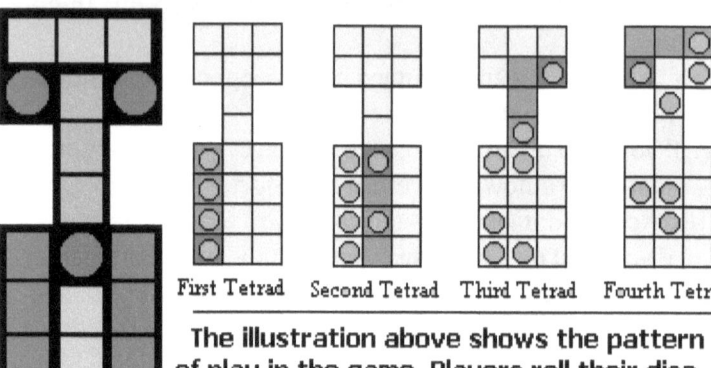

First Tetrad   Second Tetrad   Third Tetrad   Fourth Tetrad

The illustration above shows the pattern of play in the game. Players roll their dice and fill the Tetrads (4 tile groups, ending in a Flower) in the order shown. You must fill lower Tetrads before you proceed to higher ones. If you can't move some portion of your roll, you are "in chock" for that amount, and when the game is over, the person in chock loses by that amount.

The concept is simple, but in practice it is complicated and requires close attention to detail. The way players get "chocked" is shown in this illustration: the Tetrads in the head make it possible for a player to have three markers in his opponent's Tetrad, putting him in chock for one or two rolls.

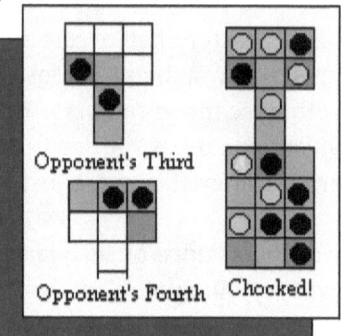

Opponent's Third

Opponent's Fourth   Chocked!

41. Ur-Chock

Of all the Chase-path games, Ur-Chock is the most complicated, the most difficult to explain, and the hardest to keep track of in play. Yet it was the simplest one to invent. My brother suggested it on the phone: "Well, you can fill each tetrad as you move your markers through the board. You would need four markers to fill the first tetrad, and two each to fill the remaining tetrads. Then they would have to go off in pairs, until the last marker jumped off." Presumably, the first player to get all seven off would win. But that's not how it turned out.

Why? Because of Chock. Being in Chock and having points scored against you became more interesting than just going off the board. You strive to get to the Head first, so you can put three markers in your opponent's final tetrad. His available spaces would soon fill up, and he would have points accumulate against him when he rolled. Space would open up as soon as you jumped off, and (as sometimes happens) he could put you in Chock. Things would clear up as the players approach the end game, when big numbers are needed to gain or maintain advantage. When they came to the final roll, whoever was in Chock would move his markers back along the Chase-path that number, and perhaps see what he would have to roll to get his last marker off. After the last move, the loser is said to be "in chock" for the number of spaces from off, for all his on-board markers. And that's the measure of his loss. But more complicated than Chock in Ur-Chock is keeping track of the order of movement. You have to fill your upper tetrads (with your two) before you can move out of a lower one, and you have to fill the lower tetrads before you can move your top pair up. So you move your markers through the Chase-path like a segmented worm. Your total roll can be moved in any sequence; you can move a marker one space, and another marker one space, then the first marker again, and the second again, until you use up your roll—and thus worm your way to the end.

However, to an accomplished Ur-player, that's like counting and stepping off in Ur-Chase, instead of adding and jumping. In Ur-Chock (especially the two-dice version) you can jump ahead to where your markers would land if you moved them up one space at a time. That practice is called "finesse." There's nothing to be gained by finesse, but it makes the game more enjoyable to seasoned players.

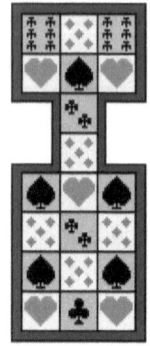

Chance Board

Ur-Chance

This Ur-game is based on various card games. The four Ur-Board suits are identified with card suits, as seen in the Chance Board. The strong suits (Gates and Flowers) become Spades and Hearts; they are the Trumps, each the exclusive property of one of the players. The Rooms (Clubs) are divided into subsuits; and Coins (Diamonds) are the odd suit.

Opening Placement

The games are played in "hands": the first to fill a suit (trumps, subsuits, or odd suit) wins the hand. Scores are accumulated toward a winning score of 21 or more. Play one-die or two-dice; they're roughly the same—except for the Grand Slam (all five subsuit numbers, worth 21 points). In two-dice it can happen almost any time; in one-die, it can occur only when you have both 2's and 6's and you roll for a one.

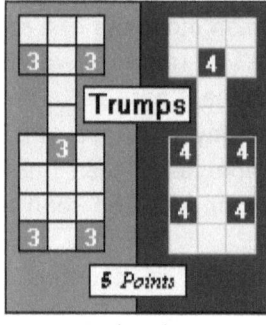

Red & Blue

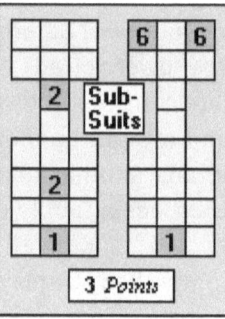

Yellow

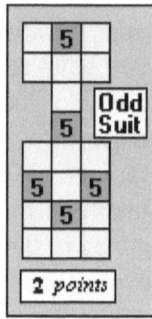

Green

42. Ur-Chance

The first decision to be made is one-die or two-dice.

The second decision is who has what trumps. There are only two choices, the 3 and the 4, and there's no strategic difference between them. Place trumps around the neck as shown in illustration.

Rules of Play

Roll and place marker(s) on open tile(s) of the suit(s) rolled.

Alternate rolls, and continue to play until someone fills a suit, which ends the hand. Record the score on a score card (a cross with the names above the crossbar, and the scores listed in order below); return to the opening placement and play the next hand. Point values of the suits are shown in the illustration.

Trumps: Only the owner's marker goes on his trump. If you roll your opponent's trump, remove a marker from his trump and place it in the odd suit.

Sub-suit: If the number you rolled has an empty tile, place your marker in it. If it is filled, remove your opponent's marker and replace it with one of yours, then put his marker in the odd suit. If only your markers fill the number, simply remove one and put it in the odd suit.

Odd suit: If you roll a 5, put a marker in the odd suit. If the odd suit is filled, replace your opponent's marker with one of yours. The same if your trump or sub-suit marker is knocked off; place it in an open odd suit tile, or replace your opponent's tile. Markers knocked off the odd suit go off the board, to be played again. Play off-board markers first.

Grand slam: If you fill the Rooms suit with your markers, you get 21 points and win the game, as discussed in the illustration.

In two-dice Ur-Chance, you can "undo" a winning score with your second die, because the roll is not over until both dice are played. This frustrating phenomenon is called the "Temporary Victory."

If you lose your sub-suits and trumps markers, you still have a chance to end the hand with a win, by filling all the Coins. Going for Coins, you can win by rolling a sub-suit number that you already have; or if your opponent removes you from a sub-suit, or from your trump. Thus your opponent can inadvertently give you the win.

Ur-Choice

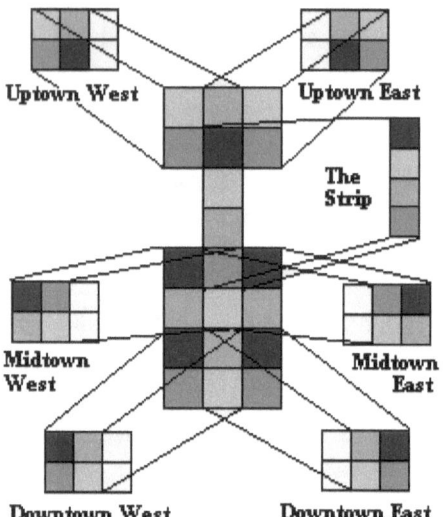

Uptown West Uptown East

The Strip

Midtown West Midtown East

Downtown West Downtown East

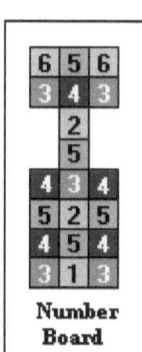

Number Board

Ur-Choice is a variant of Ur-Chance. It is a property
game, based on the seven sets of the Ur-board.
Each set is a subdivision in the city; you win the
game by filling one. The rules of play differ slightly,
but the basic difference is that in Ur-Choice you
choose where to place the number you roll. Play
to win two-out-of-three sets.

43. Ur-Choice

Just as Ur-Chase and Ur-Check are variants of the Chase-path game, Ur-Chance and Ur-Choice are variants of the Number Board game. And once again, the names precisely identify the difference between them: in Ur-Chance your place is determined by chance-- the roll of the dice; in Ur-Choice you participate by choosing where to place the marker in the suit you rolled— in which open space, in what part of the board. This choice is necessitated by the fact that you are not trying to fill the suit, but to fill one of the seven "sets" on the board.

You also choose whether to roll for two numbers, or to roll for one number and move an onboard marker from one tile to another of the same suit, or even, instead of rolling, to move two markers to open spaces of the same suits. Thus you can hold markers in any set, and keep them ready to move to the set you want to fill.

There are no trumps or odd suit. Markers knocked off the board return to play. And there is no prior placement; you move wherever you want to in the suit you roll. But there are places on the board that you want to fill, places that threaten or block the filling of sets. If you don't roll at least one of every suit, you can't win. You will have to move about to block open sets until you get what you need.

These changes in the Number Board game create a setting for intensely competitive play.

Jean and I once played Ur-Choice each evening for a month during a vacation and kept a running score, like members of a league. She took an early lead and held on. I was just starting to catch up when we had to pack and return home. In a way, I was glad. I was getting burnt out on it.

The game seems particularly well suited for a married couple.

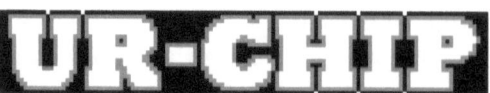

UR-CHIP

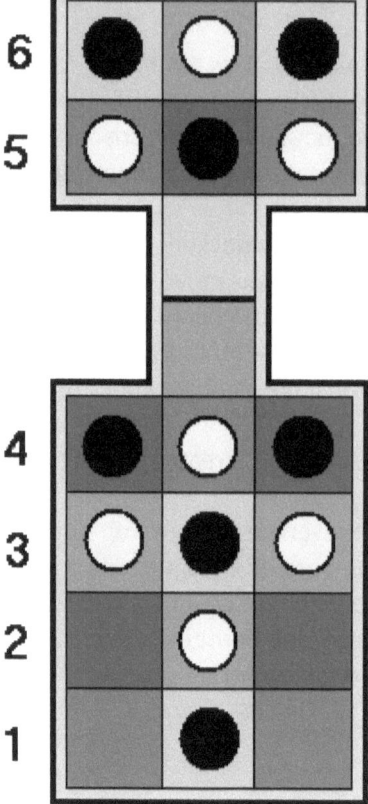

Ur-Chip is modeled after the casino games.

Each player starts out by occupying two suits in the quarters around the neck, and one center tile in the bottom quarter. The blacks have Rooms & Gates; the whites, Coins & Flowers.

The lines are numbered in ascending order: from 1 to 4 in the body, and 5 and 6 In the head. The neck is divided into two pockets, one for chips knocked off from the top, and the other for those knocked off from the bottom.

Roll one die to determine the line and move a chip from any other line to the line rolled. The object of pllay is to fill a suit.

44. Ur-Chip

Roll one die for your turn, to determine the line to put your chip on. Your chip may be taken from anywhere on the board, except the pockets. Chips are only knocked into or out of pockets.

Move only from one line to another, not within a line. Move only from one suit to another, not within a suit.

If a line is filled, knock off your opponent's chip, put it in the pocket, and replace it with yours. If you alone fill the line, choose one of your chips in that line and place it in the pocket.

If your opponent occupies the pocket for that side, replace his chip and give it to your opponent to play on any open space. If your chip is in the pocket, place your displaced chip on any open space.

A play is not over until the knocked off chips have been placed. If at the end of a play both players have a suit filled, the game is a tie.

DISCLAIMER : Ur-Corp is not responsible for failure to please.

This Ur-game is a mystery. Sometimes it doesn't work, sometimes it works beautifully. But it's such a neat design, we decided to include it. Maybe you can "honor the form" by tweaking the rules of this game. How would you improve Ur-Chip?

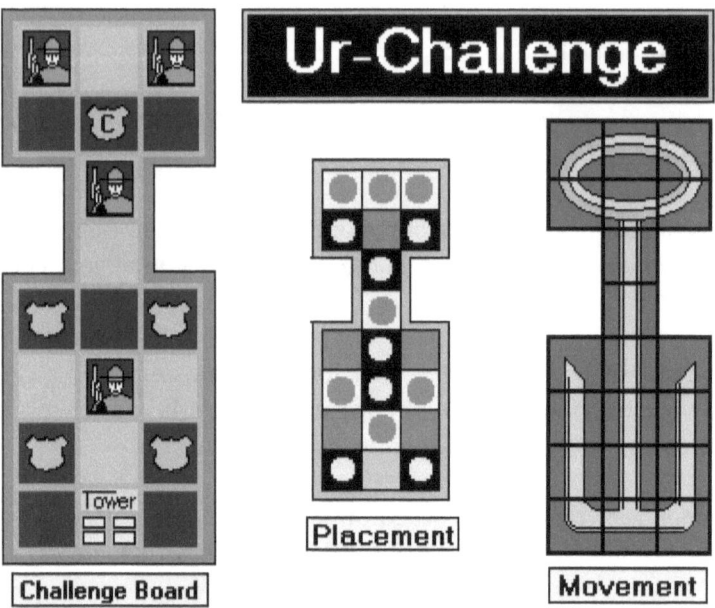

Ur-Challenge

Challenge Board

Placement

Movement

This is a cops-and-robbers game. The Ur-Board is an 8-story building, with a crowd of people in it. There are two teams of citizens, the Coins and the Flowers; each team has its pair of killers from the Rooms suit: Flowers have hit-men in the elevators, and Coins have thugs waiting for them in the top floor. The policemen, when they appear, are stationed on the Gates tiles. Headquarters are in the lobby.

45. Ur-Challenge

This is the first of the situation games, the Ur-games that resemble a scene of conflict. In this colorful game, called "gang war," the movement around the board calls to mind scenes from the movies, with killers pursuing each other and trying to elude the cops, and hapless citizens caught in the crossfire. Two gangs circle around the upper floor and turn a corner in the lobby to locate their victims. The cops are stationed in the stairwells; the chief stands guard at the elevator; and below, in the lobby, the inspector in charge of the crime unit lets pursuers pass, granting them the power of his office. The Tower is the political element in the conflict; like the cops, it represents the law; therefore, it can kill, but cannot be killed, except by a cop.

All markers are placed on the board to begin with. The teams are: five Coins plus the two Rooms in the head; and five Flowers plus the two Rooms in the center shaft. The Coins and Flowers are citizens, and the Rooms are their hired killers. But the markers do not keep that status, for they become whatever they land on in play.

The rules governing movement on the board are: Roll one die and move any marker of yours that number. Markers move back and forth along the Chase Path, but only one way in any one move. The side alleys are dead ends; you cannot move up the side if your roll is too high. You can circle around the head in any direction, but you cannot circle around completely in one move. If you roll a six, you must move out of the head.

The rules of play are: To "kill" a marker is to remove it from play. The object of play is to kill off the other team. Citizens can not kill anyone; killers can kill citizens or killers, but cannot kill cops; cops can kill anyone except another cop. The Tower (the Gate of Life) can kill cops, and cops can kill anyone in the Tower. But when the Tower is empty, anyone can kill anyone else if he passes through the Tower during that move. This is called the Power of the Tower. If a player is blocked from moving, he loses the game.

A variant of the game is called "shoot out." In that game, there are only two players at a time, situated, to begin with, in the chief's place and the Tower, six paces from each other. A six "picks off" your opponent, but if you roll less than that you have to run and shoot.

Ur-Champion

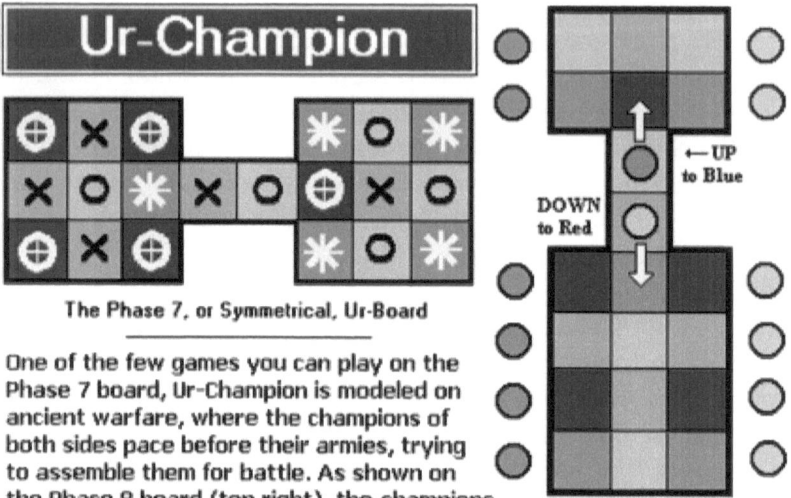

The Phase 7, or Symmetrical, Ur-Board

One of the few games you can play on the Phase 7 board, Ur-Champion is modeled on ancient warfare, where the champions of both sides pace before their armies, trying to assemble them for battle. As shown on the Phase 8 board (top right), the champions pace in opposite directions before the battle line. Whatever spot they land on, they place a marker in that suit on their side. when a champion lands between two soldiers in a line, he knocks off the enemy soldier. The object of play is to fill the six places on their side.

46. Ur-Champion

The situation in this game is primitive warfare, in which a Champion assembles his army and leads them to victory or defeat. The purpose of the Champion is to marshal his troops on the battle line. He gathers his foot soldiers (Rooms and Coins) easily enough; but then he must organize his best men, his heroes (Gates and Flowers), who are hard to find and easily lost in battle. The first army to fill its ranks wins the day.

Ur-Champion is an easy game to learn, and fun to play, for people of all ages. The trick in this game is to stay alert. You have to be on your toes just to play— first, because the Champions move in opposite directions. You must choose between the Blue and Red chips, because the Blue Champion will move up from the Neck on the first move, and continue to move from bottom to top throughout the game; and the Red Champion will move down from the Neck, and continue to move from top to bottom. You may have to remind yourself from time to time—up or down?

Second, when Champions cross, they jump over their opponent's tile and do not count that tile as part of their roll.

Third, when your Champion lands between filled positions, you knock off the enemy on that line. Some people forget to do this. In time, however, these reactions become instinctual.

This is one of those games which may be over suddenly and soon, or may drag on in mutual frustration, with each side gaining and losing ground as the Champions of both sides work to prevent their opponents from assembling.

Ur-Chuckle

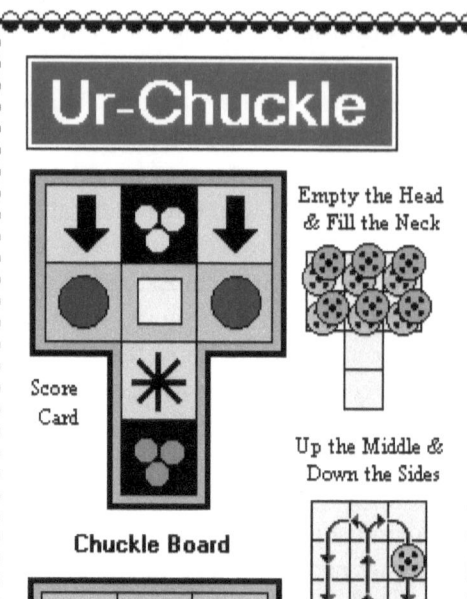

Score Card

Chuckle Board

Empty the Head & Fill the Neck

Up the Middle & Down the Sides

First ⬤ Move

Jumpover Rule

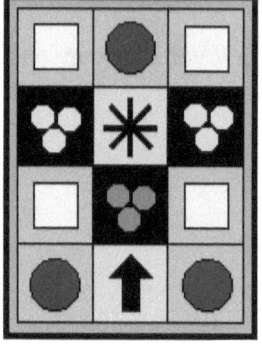

Playing Field

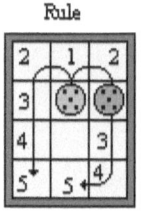

This game celebrates the Battle of the Sexes. Lots of double entendre in the rules and the names. This is a variant of the Ur-Champion game, and the winner is the first to finish.

Ur-Chuckle is used traditionally to end an Ur-nament. If the score between the players is tied, it's called a Decisive Chuckle; if the end is indeed a foregone conclusion, it's called an Academic Chuckle. It is considered the highest form of Moral Victory to win an Academic Chuckle after you have lost the Ur-nament rather badly.

47. Ur-Chuckle

Ur-Chuckle is a variant of Ur-Champion, but with its own analysis of the board, dividing it into two separate functions— the Playing Field and the Score Board.

You enter the field at the Gate of Life, and immediately encounter two distinct tiles, different from the ones around them and similar to the tiles in the neck. These initial tiles create a sub-plot to the larger narrative. Not only must you remove every marker from the head, including the two Rooms markers which are linked to only one tile in the field of play; you must also, as a sort of by-play, take two markers you have removed from other tiles and place them in the corresponding tile in the neck.

Ur-Chuckle has a special role to play in the Ur-nament (the 9 game series of Ur-games), for it is played last. As they approach this final game, the two players begin to wonder who won what games, and so to recall the Ur-nament, to find out what chance each one has of winning. If the score for the Ur-nament is tied at that point (4-4), Ur-Chuckle will be decisive, compelling; but if one player has a lead, it's all over; no need to Chuckle; the issue of the game is "academic." Under those conditions, the losing player fights for honor, for the moral victory, and such academic causes as, "At least I didn't give up." To which the only response is, "You still lost." And both players are afforded their measure of self-satisfaction.

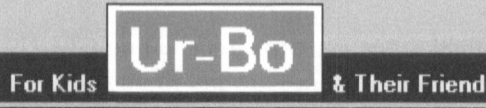

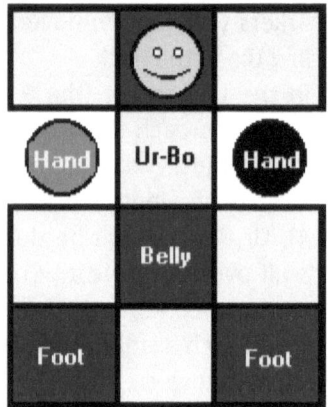

Ur-Bo Board

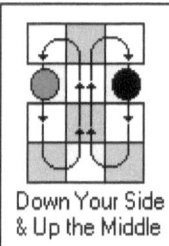

Down Your Side & Up the Middle

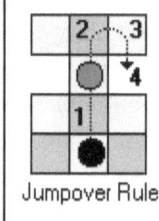

Jumpover Rule

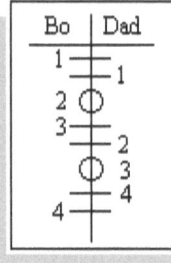

Score Board

How to Play

Roll your die and count your moves, down the side and up the middle. If you land on a dark tile, roll again, but if you land on a white tile, you have to stop. When you pass your friend's marker, you don't count the tile he's on. When you land on your "hand" tile, it means you caught the ball. Your friend has one turn to catch the ball and tie the game. If he lands on a white tile, you get a point on the score card. But if he lands on the hand tile, nobody wins. Instead, a "bubble" or circle is put on the score card, and the one who wins the next game gets one point for the bubble and one for the line. The first person to get seven points wins the whole game.

48. Ur-Bo

This is a great game to teach a kindergarten-age child. All that's required is that the child knows how to count to ten. The child's love of the game helps you teach her to cooperate with the rules, and after play to put the dice and markers in the box, and put the box and Ur-Bo away, before going on to something else, even if the child didn't finish the game. But don't just tell the child to put it away. Put your marker and die away, while she puts hers in the box, then let her show you that she knows where to store the box and board. It's part of the ritual of playing Ur-Bo.

As the child advances in skills and understanding, you can introduce her to one-die Ur-Chase. She will already have learned to jump ahead by adding instead of counting, and the larger field of play will allow her to add with higher numbers. She will also learn to adapt to different conditions, by learning, for instance, not to use the jump-over rule in Ur-Chase. For she will probably return to Ur-Bo from time to time, and use the familiar rule, knowing that it is special to that game.

It is one of the challenges of the Ur-nament to adjust mentally to the rules and principles of very different and not-so-different games. Ur-Bo introduces a person in early childhood to that habit of complex reasoning and adaptive behavior.

But the most valuable learning experience in Ur-Bo is learning how to lose. Ur-Bo is a high pressure game for a child, and she may have a hard time accepting a loss. She will learn in time, probably from your example, how to grin and bear it. To help in this matter, I put the score cards from past games in a can with the dice and markers. Gradually, on the sly, I reduce the number of her losses, so that when she reviews past scores, she seems to win most of the time. Before each game, we review past scores; and she learns not to mind losing too much, since, as the records show, most of the time she wins, and sometimes by a big margin.

49. Ur-Checkers

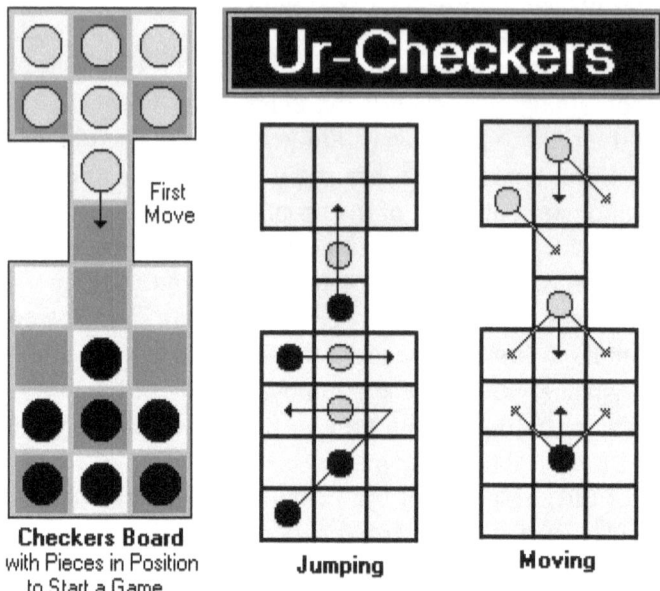

Checkers Board
with Pieces in Position
to Start a Game

First Move

Jumping

Moving

Ur-Checkers and Ur-Chess are not Ur-games: they are the Ur-Board's tribute to the games they resemble. Ur-Checkers features the neck as a narrow pass through which the markers must move to enter the field of play. It determines the first move, and the player in the body determines the conflict by how he responds to that move.

The wonder of Ur-Chess is how well the form accommodates the six pieces in Chess. There are five kings, whose combined movements cover every other position on the board. There are four pawns guarding the approach to the castle, and one in the head guarding the queens in the northern territory. There are five bishops, their diagonal movement menacing the southern kings and their castle. And the two knights in the middle can jump both the combatant pairs, kings and queens.

50. Ur-Chess

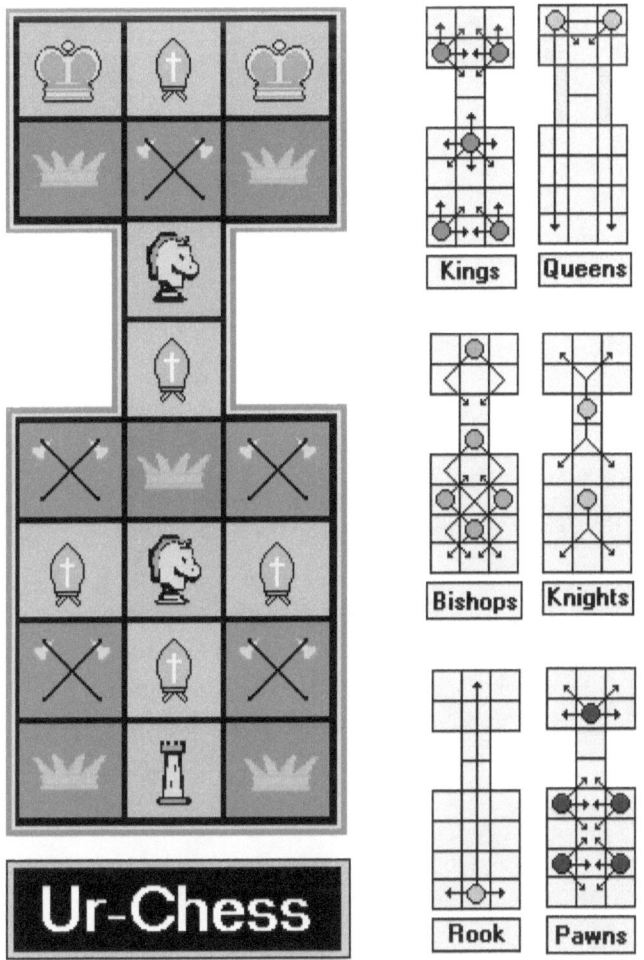

Ur-Chess

Kings

Queens

Bishops

Knights

Rook

Pawns

117

Ur-Carté

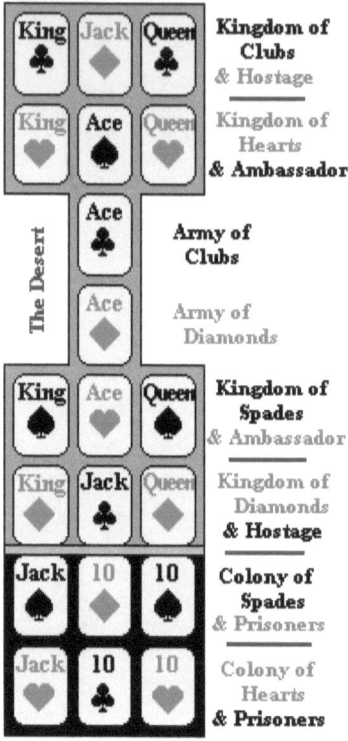

King ♣	Jack ♦	Queen ♣	**Kingdom of Clubs** *& Hostage*
King ♥	Ace ♠	Queen ♥	Kingdom of Hearts *& Ambassador*
	Ace ♣		**Army of Clubs**
	Ace ♦		Army of Diamonds
King ♠	Ace ♥	Queen ♠	**Kingdom of Spades** *& Ambassador*
King ♦	Jack ♣	Queen ♦	Kingdom of Diamonds *& Hostage*
Jack ♠	10 ♦	10 ♠	**Colony of Spades** *& Prisoners*
Jack ♥	10 ♣	10 ♥	Colony of Hearts *& Prisoners*

The Desert

This is a game of solitaire. Take the Royal Flush of the four suits of cards. Shuffle and begin to turn them over, three at a time.

Observe the following procedure:

1. Kings and Queens any time
2. Guest of a Court only when King and Queen are present
3. Armies any time
4. Armies before Prisoners, but
5. Colonial Jacks before Tens

Place the top card in the space provided for it on the Ur-board, if the rules permit it. Continue to turn over cards in that fashion until you play them all, or can't play.

51. Ur-Carté

This is the Ur-board's solitaire game. It was suggested by the four suits of playing cards, and the Royal Flush of each suit, a symbol of competition at the highest level. You will need to remove the cards from a deck and play on an Ur-board with tiles that the cards fit on.

It was easy enough to identify the suits of cards with the suits of the Ur-board. First of all, the Flowers are Hearts, not only because they are red suits, but also for their romantic associations. Besides, the central Flower tile is a symbol of the Heart. Next, the Gates are Spades, both symbols of the Underworld; the central Spade, in the head, would be the Ace of Spades, featured in cards as the most prominent design. Then, the Rooms would be Clubs, symbols of position and power. And, of course, the Diamonds would be Coins, symbols of wealth.

Now the four top lines of the Ur-Board have the four suits in their side aisles. This arrangement of suits creates kingdoms in the top lines of the board: the kingdoms of Clubs and Hearts in the head, and the kingdoms of Spades and Diamonds in the upper body. It is a system suggestive of racial division, with red and black races on either side of the neck.

Each royal court has a king and queen, seated around a visiting card. In Clubs and Diamonds, the visiting card is a Jack, representing a young heir of the enemy court, captured in battle and now a hostage. In Hearts and Spades, the visiting card is an Ace, symbol of the Ambassador from the opposite side of the neck (a desert region, separating the two states); and in the desert, the Aces symbolize the Armies of Clubs and Diamonds.

The remaining cards are the Jacks of Spades and Hearts, and the four Tens. Now the Tens are obviously not noblemen, but members of the military for their respective states. The Tens of Diamonds and Clubs are the prisoners taken by the inner states (Spades and Hearts) when the armies of their neighboring states passed through their territory; the Jacks and Tens of Spades and Hearts are the prison guards and officers in the southern colonies.

Ur-Paper Games

Ur-Dots

Remember the Formula:

12-Dash-20

Make Your Own **Ur-Crossword**

Ur-Crossword

R
WORD
S
S

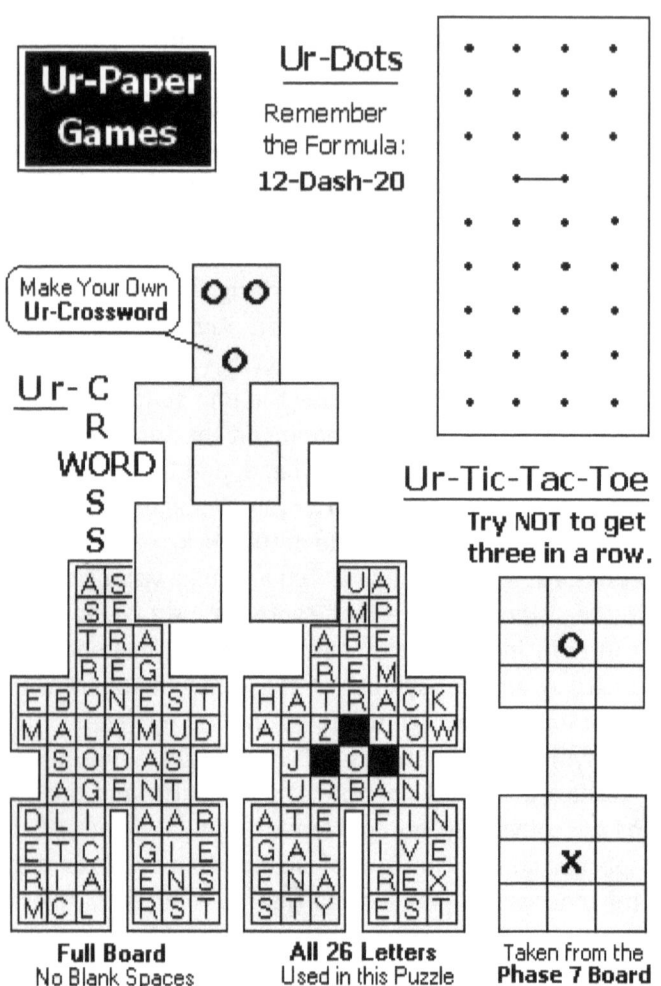

Ur-Tic-Tac-Toe

Try NOT to get three in a row.

Full Board
No Blank Spaces

All 26 Letters
Used in this Puzzle

Taken from the
Phase 7 Board

52. Ur-Paper Games

Here are a few paper games suggested by the shape and nature of the Ur-board. They represent an attempt to improve the popular pencil-and-paper games played by people.

The first, **Ur-Tic-Tac-Toe**, is played on a "symmetrical Ur-board" (the Phase 7 board, but without only two symbols). The O and X symbols are retained exactly where they were, in the center of the box above and below the neck. Then the two players begin to set down their Os and Xs, anywhere on the board, trying *not* to get three-in-a-row. Toward the end, it becomes difficult to avoid getting three-in-a-row as you begin to run out of options. You have to prepare to go the distance, by leaving yourself enough empty spaces.

The second Ur-Papergame is the game of dots, played by kids all over the country in idle hours after school. Usually, the game sprawls all over the page and creates a smudged and wrinkled field when the squares begin to fill. But **Ur-Dots** reduces the field to a small manageable size, which can be reproduced by the simple formula "12-dash-20," indicating how to arrange the dots, from the top down. The dash in the middle joins the two middle dots in the neck, separating two areas of play, a small and a large.

And finally, there is **Ur-Crossword**, made by drawing three interlocking Ur-boards, with all their squares. Beginners can use the internal design made by blacking in the Flowers tiles (so there's not too much interlocking of words) For experts, there is the whole puzzle without any black squares. The typical Ur-Crossword has three or four black squares in the middle of the triple-Ur-board form, challenging the puzzle-maker to interlock six-, seven-, and eight- letter words.

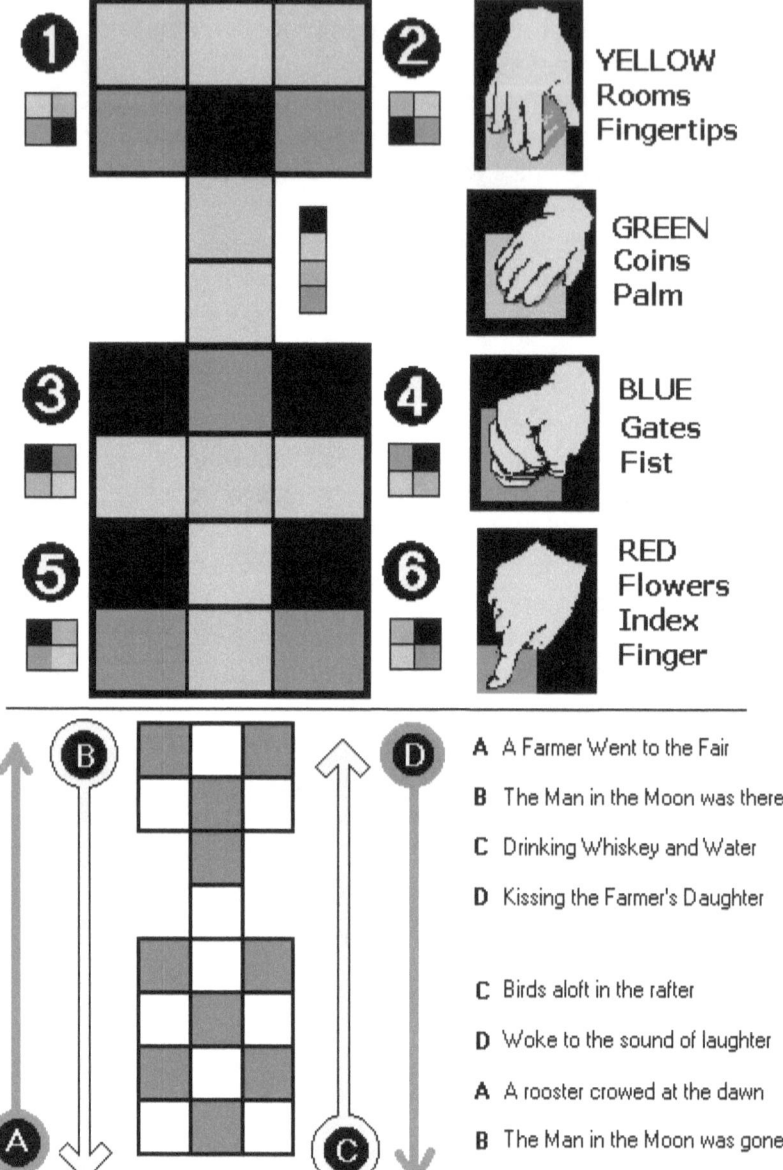

❶ **❷**

❸ **❹**

❺ **❻**

YELLOW
Rooms
Fingertips

GREEN
Coins
Palm

BLUE
Gates
Fist

RED
Flowers
Index
Finger

A A Farmer Went to the Fair

B The Man in the Moon was there

C Drinking Whiskey and Water

D Kissing the Farmer's Daughter

C Birds aloft in the rafter

D Woke to the sound of laughter

A A rooster crowed at the dawn

B The Man in the Moon was gone

53. Ur-Party Games

Ur-Chairs is the ur-version of "Musical Chairs." It is played at a party by seven players. Each one takes a turn at each position, beginning with the Caller, and passing on to 1 in the head, and 2 across from it, and on to 3 in the body, and all the way around to 4, and on to 5 and 6 on the bottom, and from 6 to Caller, and on to 1, etc. So, everybody is moving around the table, going from place to place to set up for the next call. There are six players around the board, but only five tiles of each color. So, when caller suddenly calls the color, there's a mad scramble of hands seeking to occupy tiles of that color, but— you have to occupy the tile in the hand position appropriate to it. Each color has its own hand gesture.

Players must remove rings from playing hand.

Among those familiar with the Form, you can add the further complication of calling the colors by their suit names— Rooms, Coins, Gates, and Flowers.

* * *

Ur-Scotch is the ur-version of "Hop Scotch." It is not a game. It's a performance. A child practices it until she or he can do it smoothly, as a kind of dance. You have to recite the poem at the pace you jump, hitting the stressed syllables with two feet and skipping to the anapest in the neck. You go up the Blue to begin the poem, and down the White to get the rhyme, then up the White, and down the Blue. That's the first stanza. The second stanza lines occur in a slightly different order.

The ideal performance is soft and fast, landing light on your feet and reciting at a casual pace. Practice, practice.

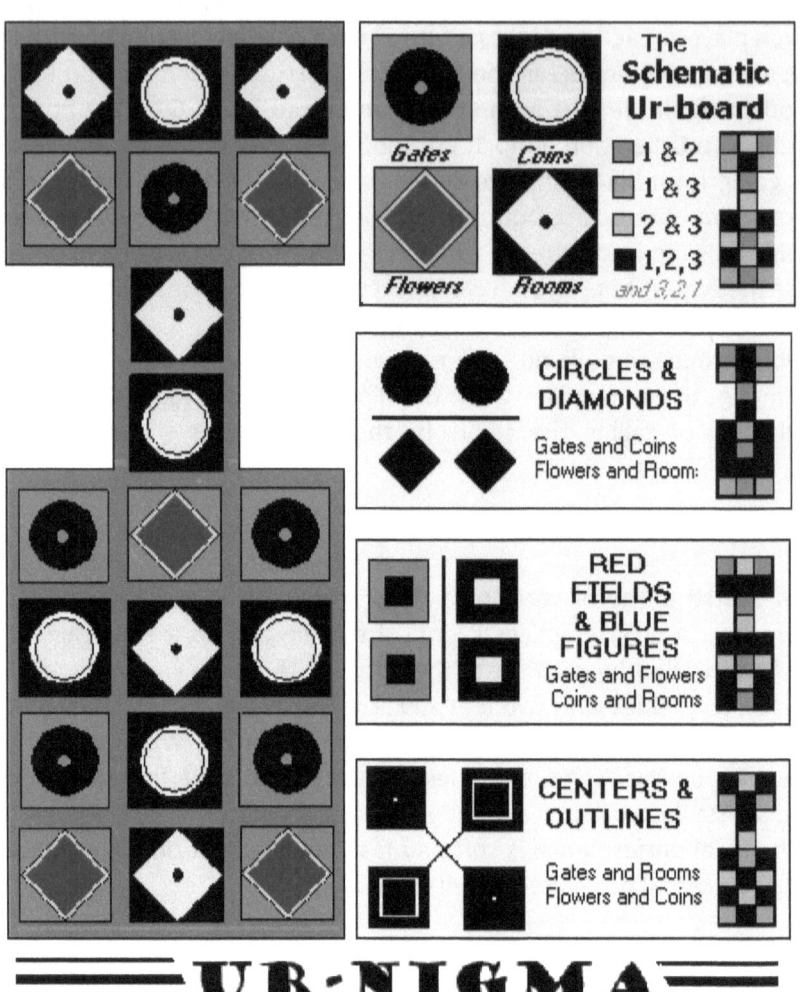

The Schematic Ur-board

Gates *Coins*

◼ 1 & 2
◼ 1 & 3
◻ 2 & 3
◼ 1,2,3

Flowers *Rooms* *and 3,2,1*

CIRCLES & DIAMONDS

Gates and Coins
Flowers and Room:

RED FIELDS & BLUE FIGURES

Gates and Flowers
Coins and Rooms

CENTERS & OUTLINES

Gates and Rooms
Flowers and Coins

UR·NIGMA

54. Ur-Nigma

This game is an initiation into the mysteries of the Ur-board. It comes in the form of a puzzle, based on Ur-board design, a puzzle which, when solved, reveals the logic of the Ur-board.

But you will enjoy working this puzzle _only once_: when it is fresh. Once you have worked it, it is no longer a puzzle. You can only gaze at the familiar chart and watch as your eye organizes the scene into a meaningful design.

You have become an initiate.

As such, you have a responsibility toward those who have not yet solved the puzzle, especially someone who is working on it. Be thoughtful and taciturn: Do not interfere with a beginner's right to solve the puzzle herself. Do not explain it to anyone, nor ask anyone to explain it to you.

If a beginner insists on sharing his insights with you, you should listen in silence and agree with everything.

Everyone who is curious about Ur-Nigma should discover the rules of the game and its Analytic Chart by studying the directions and solving the puzzle.

55. The Ur-Sonnet

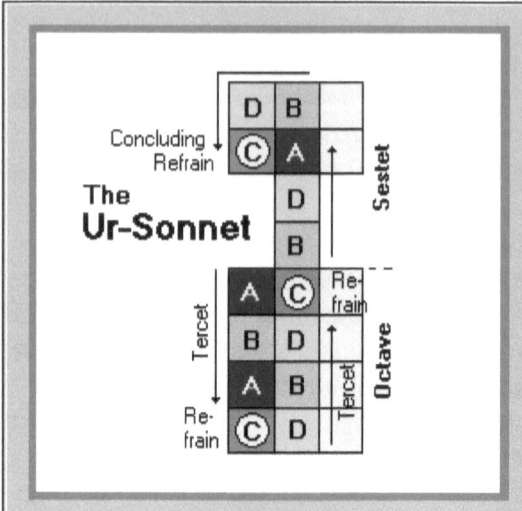

1. Ur-Chase

In Eden, when a simply perfect day
Declined toward yet another splendid night,
Adam would call his sexless wife to play
    Ur-Chase, the game of kings and king of games!

In Ur, too, when the Great Man had to crawl
Into his grave, his subjects eased his plight
With various amusements— best of all
    Ur-Chase, the game of kings and king of games!

Nothing deprived our fathers of their right
To praeternatural happiness: the Fall
Could not deject them, nor the Spring dismay.
If routed from their beds and put to flight,
They'd play Ur-Chase— and that is why we call
    Ur Chase the game of kings and king of games!

So, the Ur-board leads us on, from play to art, from art to philosophy, from symbolism to prophecy, from fun to faith, all in one leap.

I had noticed the similarity between the Ur-Board and the sonnet, both as Forms for the production of art, and as examples of harmonious and balanced design. The Octave and Sestet division, the 8 to 6 ratio, is found there in the center aisle and side aisle.

All you have to do is move down the first Tetrad, and up the center shaft to the top, and down the side. The Tetrads in the body form two quatrains, with two tercets in the neck and head.

Each quatrain has a tercet followed by a C-rhyme; and the tercets in the head were just about to conclude with their own rhyme, when a final C-rhyme intervened. It tells me that the C-line is not merely a rhyme, but a whole line repeated as a refrain. The Form is therefore not just a sonnet, but a new and unique verse form. To test the effectiveness of the refrain as a device, I produced what surely must be the first Ur-sonnets in the history of the world-- this world, at least; so for this historic premiere performance, I chose as theme the first 3 Ur-games-- Ur-Chase, Ur-Check, and Ur-Chock.

I hope you enjoy them.

2. Ur-Check

Though fools will forfeit health and happiness
To be the envy of their foolish friends,
I'm not impressed by failure or success.
   I judge a man by how he plays Ur-Check.

What man can say he has truly understood
The moral issues or the social trends?
One person's evil is another's good.
   I judge a man by how he plays Ur-Check.

To Ur is human. Wisdom recommends
That lest we perish in our pride, we should
Leave it to Heaven to condemn or bless.
Ours is the means, to God belong the ends.
And therefore, for the sake of brotherhood,
   I judge a man by how he plays Ur-Check.

3. Ur-Chock

Behold the priests of Anu, short and fat,
Their infant pates emblazoned by the Sun,
As hunkered atop the towering ziggurat
   They cast Ur-Chock for an oracle from God.

And lo, the kings of Ur, their majesties
Consigned to the grave, their weary courses run
Yet in the darkness on their royal knees
   They cast Ur-Chock for an oracle from God.

No wonder, then, that we who play for fun,
Feeling the strain of life's uncertainties
With each roll of the dice, and dreading that,
Agree to play but one game--- only one.
In Sumer, to instruct was not to please.
   They cast Ur-Chock for an oracle from God.

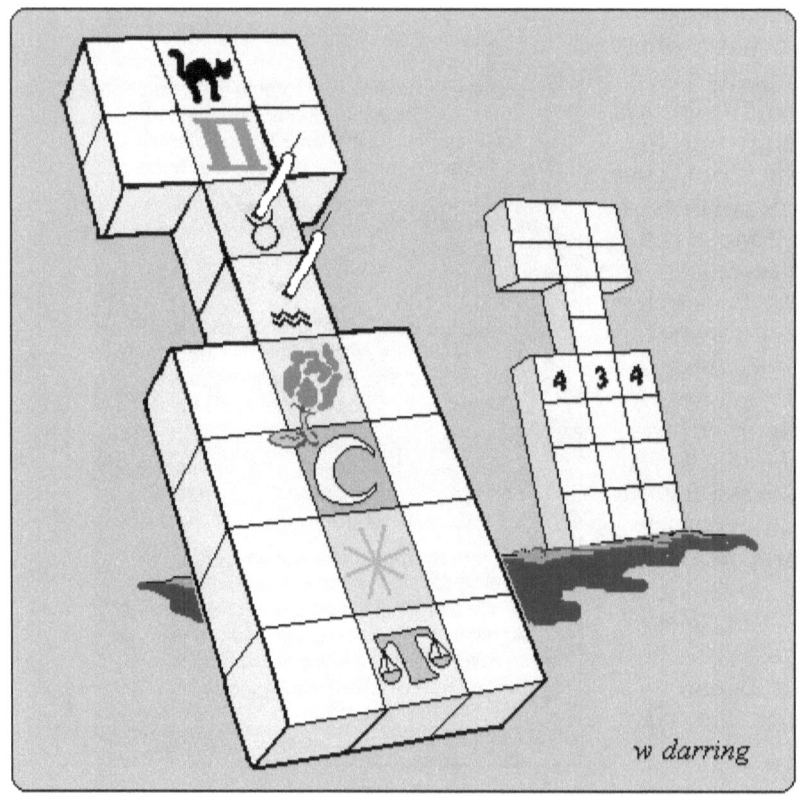

w darring

56. The Wizard's Signature (Written in Fate's Hand)

This book of symbols and games contains my interpretation of the Ur-board, and my opinions about everything else. And who am I? Why— I am the *Wizard of Ur*. For some reason, I was chosen for this task. So— there, I've done it.

If there is any question of my authenticity as an intermediary, an interpreter— I refer my readers to the Ur-board itself. There, in the design of the game board, you will find a secret message to validate my claim.

You remember the tribute to dice on the Number Board— the eleven 7's, and the seven 11's? You remember the totals of the two halves of the board— 34 in the head, and 43 in the body? Well, those were my signature. I was born on November 7, 1934 (that's 11-7-34) and the number assigned to me at school, which became my identifying number, was 43. When I saw these numbers appear as a consequence of the Number Board, I knew the Ur-board had confirmed my role.

But such coincidences are, no doubt, more impressive to those who experience them, than to those who must be told about them. So the Ur-board has prepared an additional correspondence that might satisfy the skeptic, and make him, perhaps for a moment, doubt his own doubt.

When Jean and I were married, we decided to have a large family, and Jean even specified— eight children. Well, by 1966, we had our eight children, who had arrived in this order— four girls, two boys, and two girls. In keeping with the X and Y gene makeup, the girls should be symbolized by 3-tile lines, and the boys by 1-tile lines. And when you arrange them that way, in an upward progression— our family forms an Ur-board.

How otherwise could the prophetic Oversoul symbolize its approval of my work, five thousand years before my birth, save by making a recognizable sign—a birth date, a magic number board, a family form? And here they are, all three. My foretold signature.

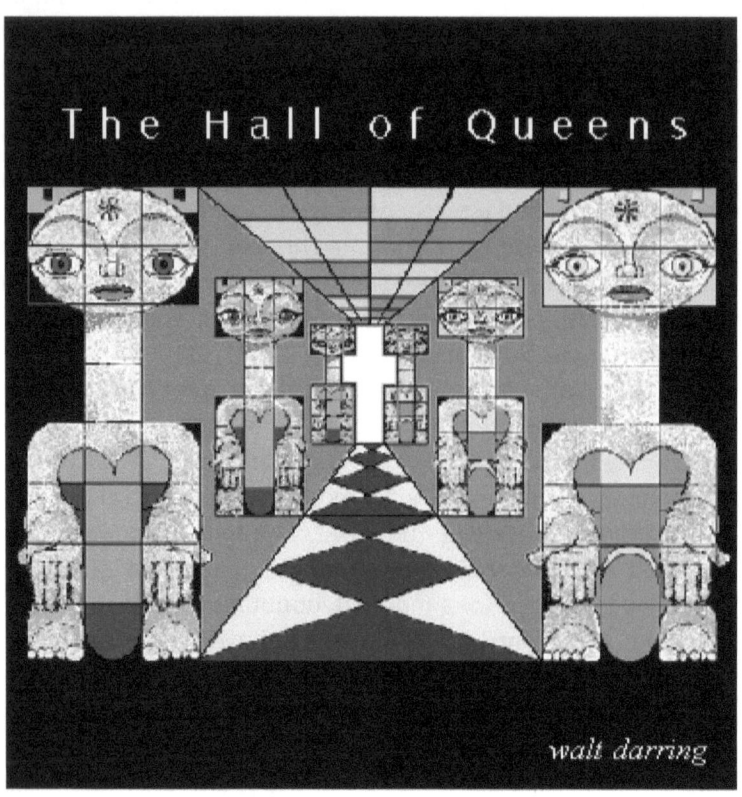

The Hall of Queens

walt darring

57. A Fond Farewell

I leave you, my Ur-chins, with this vision of the Afterlife. It is my
contribution to the cause of "honoring the Form." Here you see
the path the soul takes, as it is ushered into paradise between
the rows of Earth's mothers, symbols of Beauty, Love, and Hope.